# KNIVES & SPOONS

# KNIVES & SPOONS

A MEMOIR

LUIS J. GOMEZ

PERMUTED
PRESS

A PERMUTED PRESS BOOK
ISBN: 979-8-89565-102-5
ISBN (eBook): 979-8-89565-103-2

Knives & Spoons


Cover art by Conroy Accord

This book, as well as any other Permuted Press publications, may be purchased in bulk quantities at a special discounted rate. Contact orders@permutedpress.com for more information.

All people, locations, events, and situations are portrayed to the best of the author's memory. While all of the events described are true, many names and identifying details have been changed to protect the privacy of the people involved.



PERMUTED
PRESS

Permuted Press
New York • Nashville

permutedpress.com

Published in the United States of America

2 3 4 5 6 7 8 9 10

This book is dedicated to my son, James.
You are the reason I keep moving forward and the reason I work as hard as I do. Everything I've built, and everything I will continue to build, is for you.

I also want to honor the memory of my parents,
Denise M. Painter and Hector L. Gomez.
Life with you was complicated, but you are both part of me, and your stories live on through mine.

To my family, friends, and everyone who has supported me on this path—thank you for helping me live a story worth telling.

# TABLE OF CONTENTS

# FOREWORD

## BY ROBERT KELLY

If you're reading this, it means you've either heard of Luis J. Gomez or you're about to find out why he's impossible to ignore. Either way, you're in for a hell of a story. This book isn't about comedy or podcasting or making it in a brutal business. It's about survival, family, friendship, and beating the odds. It's about building a life from nothing and defending it with everything you've got.

Luis didn't get handed any easy breaks in life. His father was murdered when he was a kid, and his mother passed away from drugs later in his life. Most people wouldn't have made it through that kind of loss and chaos, let alone built anything out of it. But Luis didn't just survive—he refused to give up on himself, on his family, or on his friends. Through every setback, every betrayal, every fight that left him bloody but not broken, he kept swinging. That's something you can't teach; that's something you're born with.

The first time I met Luis, he was walking down my street in New York City shirtless, on his way to beat up his roommate. Fists clenched, eyes wild—he looked like a man on a mission.

But I didn't see some psycho looking to smash someone's face in. I saw a man trying to figure out how to live by a code, even when the world didn't give him one to start with. I saw myself.

And that instinct to protect, to fix what's broken, is something Luis has carried with him every step of the way. That's what people miss about him. He's never been a bad person doing bad things. He's a good person doing whatever it takes to keep the wolves at bay, even if it means becoming a wolf himself every now and then.

When I first met Luis, I saw a lot of myself in him—the attitude, the fire, the walls built high enough to keep out the world. But it was more than that. There was something in his eyes that I recognized instantly; a kid who grew up without a father, figuring out how to be a man on his own terms. It's a look you can't fake, and one you don't ever forget.

Luis doesn't quit on his friends, even when they might deserve it. He's the kind of guy who, if you're in a jam at two in the morning, you don't even have to ask. That loyalty comes from years of doing it alone, of knowing what it's like to have no one pick up the phone. When you've built your life from the ground up, brick by brick, you value the people who stuck by you—and Luis has never forgotten who was there. He's built a family out of friends, and that loyalty runs deep.

Over the years, I've seen Luis level up in every way possible. In the middle of running a bunch of businesses, organizing one of the biggest and best comedy festivals in the country, and hosting some of the most insane and successful podcasts out there, he's turned into one of the funniest motherfuckers working today.

His stand-up isn't just stronger—it's lethal. He's honed his voice, sharpened his instincts, and put in the kind of work that most people only talk about. It's been something else, watching him go from a raw kid with a chip on his shoulder to a killer on stage who commands the room.

And then there's being a father. Witnessing Luis evolve into the dad he is today has been one of the most impressive transformations I've ever seen. He took everything he didn't get growing up and made sure his son never had to question if he was loved, if he was protected, if he mattered. That's not an easy thing to do when you've spent your whole life fighting to prove that you matter too.

But Luis didn't just rise to the occasion—he blew past it. He's the kind of dad who shows up, who listens, and who teaches his son to stand up for himself and to be himself without fears. For a kid who never had a father to show him the way, that's nothing short of incredible. He's the father we should all strive to be.

I've watched Luis turn every obstacle into fuel and every loss into a lesson. Through it all, he's become one of the best men I know, one of the best brothers I could ask for, and one of the strongest human beings I've ever met. I'm proud to call him family.

This book isn't a victory lap. Luis isn't done. This is about what it takes to survive in a world that doesn't cut you any breaks. It's about pushing through, even when you're not sure where you're going to end up, and becoming the kind of father you never had, the kind of friend you always needed. It's proof that no matter how messed up the past was, it doesn't get to define how you chose to live your future.

So, turn the page and get ready for a story that's messy and brutal and hilarious all at once. Because if there's one thing Luis J. Gomez has proven, it's that you can't count out the kid with nothing to lose and everything to fight for.

—Robert Kelly

# PROLOGUE

Dear Doggies,

Thank you for picking up *Knives & Spoons*. That means the world to me.

Right now, I'm sitting in my living room, killing time before taking my family on a trip to Rome and Venice. A few days ago, I filmed my third comedy special in Tampa. I'm sipping on a cup of testosterone-boosting coffee that I conceptualized and brought to market. And, in about an hour, I have a call about expanding Skankfest, the biggest comedy festival in the world, to an international location.

I say all that not to brag, but because none of this was supposed to happen. Not for me.

When I was a kid, I never thought I'd leave Rockland County. If you'd told me back then what I'd grow up to become, the places I'd see, the people I'd meet, the things I'd build, I would've laughed in your face. Because I never had a plan. I never had a blueprint. I wasn't supposed to succeed.

The truth is, I was dealt a rough hand. You'll see that in these pages. You'll read about the trauma, the poverty, the violence, the loss, and the hustle it took just to survive. But this isn't a sob story. I'm not complaining. I have no regrets. I wouldn't change a single moment because every awful thing that happened was part of the path that brought me here.

This book is a collection of core memories, the building blocks of who I am today. Some are painful. Some are ridiculous. Some are funny in ways that might make you feel guilty for laughing. But all of them are real.

I'm proud of the man I've become. That's not something I could've said for most of my life. Today, I've got an amazing career, a brilliant son, loyal friends and family, and the best fan base in the world. You guys.

So, if there's a message in all of this, it's this: We don't control the hand we're dealt, but we do control how we play it. I didn't get 2-7 off-suit, but it sure as hell wasn't pocket aces either. More like pocket fours. No one really knows what to do with pocket fours.

Raise. Check. Bluff. Cheat. Do what you've got to do. Just keep playing.

This book isn't the whole story. It's the first half. When they first approached me about writing a book, the plan was to focus on everything I've built. All the wins. But I pulled back. That's not the book I needed to write yet. Because the most important part of any journey is the start, and I'm just getting started.

Thanks for being a part of the ride.

—Luis J. Gomez

# CHAPTER 1
# DOOKIE

If you've been following me for years, you already know I had what most would call a fucked-up childhood. I dealt with a lot of bullshit from my mother, family members, teachers, bullies, and plenty of people I was supposed to trust. Every story in this book is just another notch in the timeline that led me to this exact moment, writing these words.

And I wouldn't change a thing.

The good, the bad, it all had to happen. Everything had to happen just the way it did, to end up right here.

Hopefully, in these pages, you'll learn a few things you didn't know about me, and maybe gain some new insight into the things you did.

And if you're new here...buckle up.

I was born on April 1, 1982. Yes, April Fools' Day. While the masses were playing pranks, I was making my grand entrance into the world. I have an older sister, Jeniece E. Gomez, born just a little over two years earlier on March 26, 1980, and I came into this world thanks to my mother,

Denise M. Painter, and my dad, Hector L. Gomez. Oh, and I was born at St. Joe's Hospital in Paterson, New Jersey. So, if you're ever in the area, feel free to stop by and pay homage to the cultural landmark where this April Fool was unleashed.

Honestly, when I think back to my earliest childhood memories, there aren't a whole lot to go on. Just a few flashes here and there that don't really form a coherent picture. But there's one memory that stands out as my first actual memory. I must have been two or three years old. I remember sitting for what felt like hours on one of those rocking horses with springs attached to a metal base.

It was one of those classic toys from almost anyone's childhood. But here's the thing: I wasn't sitting there because I loved the gentle rocking motion or because it was some magical, childhood moment. I was sitting there because I was trapped.

Our house was essentially a minefield, and those mines were dog shit. Literal dog shit.

We had a black lab or some other big black dog. It was huge compared to my sister and I. His name was Dookie.

The reason his name was Dookie? This dog would take massive shits all over the house. He could have just as easily been named Shithouse. Dookie just sounded better.

Instead of actually cleaning up the mess, my parents basically just decided: *You know what? This is our reality now.* The dog shit was going to become part of the décor. They gave up. No effort to fix it, no shame about it…it was just the new normal. And I've carried that memory with me ever since: sitting there on that horse, scared of the dog, completely surrounded by little piles of shit.

It wasn't until a few years ago that I found newspaper articles about my dad's murder:

> *HEADLINE: TWO TEENS INDICTED FOR MURDER IN STABBING DEATH*
> *"A Passaic County grand jury yesterday indicted two teenagers on murder charges in the stabbing death of a Paterson man last year. Superior Court Judge Howard H. Kestin ruled in November that the defendants, Andre Hernandez, 17, and Cristino Feliciano, 15, both of Paterson, must be tried as adults because there was insufficient evidence that they could be rehabilitated before they are 19. They are charged in the death of Hector Gomez, 28, on September 13. Gomez was stabbed to death after an argument in front of Johnny's Lounge at Market and Prospect streets. At the time, Hernandez was on a weekend leave from the Skillman Training School for Boys in Montgomery Township, where he was serving a two—year sentence for drug possession. Paterson police have said that the boys and a 14-year-old girl were walking down Prospect Street at about 1 a.m. that morning when they encountered Gomez. Detective Robert Smith said at a probable cause hearing last fall that Hernandez claimed Gomez was standing with several prostitutes and when the three approached, told them to 'get off my block.' In his testimony at the time, Smith gave the following account: Gomez*

*and Hernandez got into an argument and Gomez hit Hernandez, knocking him down. The youths went to Feliciano's home to get a kitchen knife. Feliciano gave Hernandez a butcher knife with a nine—inch blade. About 2 a.m., they returned to Prospect and Market streets. Gomez was standing in front of the bar, as were other people. Hernandez challenged Gomez to a fight. 'Go home,' Gomez reportedly told him. 'You're too young to be out here, youngblood.' Angered by Gomez's taunt, the youth stabbed him in the side with the knife. He then threw the knife under a car and fled. Feliciano picked up the knife, wiped it off, and brought it back to his house. Gomez died at St. Jospeh's Hospital and Medical Center in Paterson at 2:12 a.m.*

*Hernandez was arrested at 9:40 that morning at his home. Feliciano was picked up early the next morning at his home. They remain in the county's juvenile detention center. In addition to murder, they are charged with possession of a weapon for an unlawful purpose."*

*HEADLINE: GIRLFRIEND OF VICTIM QUESTIONS RELEASE OF STABBING SUSPECT*

*"Paterson—Denise Painter, fighting back tears, said authorities should have kept the suspect accused of stabbing her boyfriend to death in jail Friday night instead of releasing him for*

*the weekend on good behavior. The 17-year-old suspect had been serving a two-year sentence in a juvenile detention center in southern New Jersey but was allowed to leave for the weekend after being deemed non-violent by authorities. Less than a day after his release, however, he was arrested and accused of fatally stabbing Hector Gomez, Painter's boyfriend.*

*James Stabile, a spokesperson for the state Department of Corrections, said the suspect, whose name was not released, was serving time for possession of illegal drugs with intent to distribute and was a model inmate at the Skillman Training School. In contrast, Paterson Detective William Van Der Veen said the juvenile suspect had told him after being arrested on Saturday that he was in the detention center on assault and drug charges.*

*'They let him (the suspect) out, but they should have kept him in jail.' said Painter, interviewed Monday on Market Street near the site of her boyfriend's death. Two other juveniles, a 14-year-old girl and a 15-year-old boy, were arrested on Sunday in connection with the stabbing death. Their names also withheld. The 17-year-old is charged with homicide, the 15-year-old with aiding and abetting the crime, and the 14-year-old is said to be a material witness.*

*All three were reportedly being held in the Passaic County Juvenile Detention Center in Wayne on Monday. They were scheduled for a probable cause hearing before a Superior Court Judge today. A detective familiar with the case said it is possible the homicide suspect will be tried as an adult. Stabile said the juvenile suspect was given the pass because he was not deemed 'assaultive,' meaning he had no history of violence. He said the juvenile was released under a program designed to keep inmates in touch with families and support groups to prepare for their permanent release. Stabile said the suspect had served nine months of a two-year term and had been on such good behavior that, in May, he was given a 45-day reduction in his sentence. Further, Stabile said the suspect could have been released on parole before Christmas this year after serving only half his sentence. Another detective said the suspect is charged with stabbing Gomez at a Prospect Street parking lot after the two had fought earlier in the night.*

*Gomez, 28, was in the area just 'hanging out,' according to his girlfriend. She said Gomez and the suspect fought briefly before the suspect left the area and allegedly returned with a knife and stabbed Gomez once in the side. Painter said that after being stabbed, Gomez staggered up the street to the intersection of Market Street where he collapsed on the curb."*

*HEADLINE: TWO TEENAGERS PLEAD GUILTY*

*"PATERSON—A teenager, who was on weekend leave from a correctional institution, and his accomplice pleaded guilty Wednesday to the September 13, 1986, stabbing death of a 28-year-old man.*

*Andre Hernandez, 17, pleaded guilty to aggravated manslaughter and will face a maximum term of twenty years. Crestiano Feliciano, 16, pleaded guilty to a charge of aiding in an aggravated manslaughter and faces a maximum sentence of seven years. Both will be sentenced January 15th.*

*Hernandez told the court that he was serving a drug and assault sentence as a juvenile at Skillman Training School and was released on a weekend pass. Hernandez said he and Feliciano were walking in the area of Prospect and Market streets with a 14-year-old girl when Hector Gomez of North Fourth Street made a derogatory remark about the girl.*

*After a fist fight with Gomez, Hernandez said he went to Feliciano's home and grabbed a kitchen knife. Hernandez said he found Gomez and stabbed him once in the side. Gomez collapsed in front of a crowd outside Johnny's Lounge shortly before 2 a.m."*

# CHAPTER 2
# BENSON STREET

Another harsh truth I had to come to terms with was that my mom was a prostitute and a drug addict. It's something that has been openly acknowledged by older members of the family in the years since, but that's not how I found out. The first time I realized my mother was a prostitute I must have been three or four years old. We were down the shore in Jersey, and there was this older guy, Tom, who was hanging around.

He had always been involved in my mother's life since she was a little girl. Tom was also my sister's godfather. One day, I walked in on my mom having sex with Tom. And I remember that even though I was just a little kid, I had this situational awareness like I knew it was for money. I thought, "Oh, that's not love, that's not pleasure." I remember thinking it was a transaction.

I learned what prostitution was through a logical thought process while seeing it play out in real time with my own eyes. Nobody told me what a prostitute was. Nobody told me that was even a thing. But I saw it happen, and I went, "Oh, he's paying her to do that."

(And as a side note: My mom didn't work for my father. He wasn't her pimp. They were two independent contractors. I guess the chances of them meeting each other was low-class serendipity.)

From what I understand, my mom was around fifteen or sixteen when she met my father, who was about nineteen at the time. My mother was Italian-Irish. She had light skin. She also had dark hair and light eyes which is always a sign of trouble in my experience. Women with dark hair and light eyes are always the craziest. A lot of people would say she looked like Demi Moore when I was a kid.

When she met my father, he was already married. According to my mother, his parents forced him to marry a woman named Carmen after he got her pregnant when he was still a teenager. But that didn't stop him from going back and forth between Carmen and my mother for years. He ended up having kids with both of them. Our families overlap in age.

He was twenty-eight when he died, and my mom was still really young. I believe she was already using drugs, specifically heroin, and she eventually got him hooked, too. She was a bad influence on him. By eighteen, she was pregnant with my sister, and by twenty, she had me.

I don't really speak with my half-brothers and half-sisters, my father's other kids. Some of them have reached out over the years, but we don't have much of a relationship. It's a bit complicated. My mother hated his wife, Carmen, and maybe subconsciously she instilled an "us versus them" mentality that I still hold onto to this day.

That's the world my father created. Bouncing back and forth between two lives. Building two families. As you'll read later on, this ends up being an inherited trait.

My mother once told me a story about her throwing Carmen through a window, but who knows if that's true. My mother was a habitual liar. I learned the phrase "habitual liar" from my mother. It's something she would regularly call me throughout my childhood. I think she was projecting. She also told us that she was friends with Madonna and spent a night partying with Lawrence Taylor. Maybe the Lawrence Taylor story is true. That guy partied hard.

When my mother got pregnant with us, she'd stop using drugs, but as soon as she gave birth, she'd go right back to it. She never breastfed us because she couldn't stay off heroin long enough. She'd bounce between being strung out on the streets and getting temporarily clean. She was trying, but the drugs had a grip on her. Kicking the habit while raising two kids was more than she could handle.

When my sister started kindergarten in Paterson, NJ, she was the only White kid in a class made up of entirely black kids. And my mother, for all of the bad stuff about her, had the sense to know that she didn't want her kids going to school in Paterson. So, she ended up having my sister go live with my Aunt Anna Marie and my Great-Grandma Rose, in Rockland County, NY.

When I was three years old, my mom was arrested for drug possession—we assume. We're not really sure. Either way, she was forced to go to inpatient rehab, and DYFS (the Division of Youth and Family Services) ended up taking me.

They called my Aunt Anna Marie and my Grandma Rose, who agreed to take me in. I ended up living apart from my mother for about two years while she still struggled in Paterson to get clean. It was during this time that my father was murdered.

I thank God for my Aunt Anna Marie, who is actually my mother's aunt. She's a true saint. She helped raise both my son and my niece, and she helped raise my mother, her brothers, myself, and my sister. She's dedicated her life to caring for multiple generations of kids, even though she never had children of her own. She truly devoted herself to raising us.

As for my Great-Grandma Rose, she wasn't as kind. She had a lot of medical issues, and was constantly in physical pain. She was just mean to me. Just a crabby old Italian lady. I'm not sure if she ever actually loved me. They lived at 52 Benson Street, in West Haverstraw, New York, in a very poor, predominantly White neighborhood.

It wasn't quite a trailer park, but it was rundown and low-income. Most of the houses were split-levels, with two or three families living in each. The place was full of rough, working-class people, and a lot of what you'd call "white trash" kids. Then there was me, the only little Brown kid in the neighborhood, which helped shaped my sense of identity.

I remember the first day of kindergarten in 1987, when I was five years old. I went to West Haverstraw Elementary School. They let the kids choose where to sit, and what was interesting was that all the kids, whether they were Latino, Black, or White, naturally gravitated toward sitting with others who looked like them. It was a sort of self-segregation that happened without anyone even thinking about it.

But then there was me, sitting at the "white" table with the White kids. It was confusing for me. I was having identity issues. My dad was Puerto Rican, but my mom was Italian-Irish and I was being raised by my White family in a predominantly White neighborhood. The Puerto Rican side of my family still lived in Paterson and in the surrounding areas in Jersey, so it was mostly my White relatives who raised me.

Growing up, I was surrounded by poverty and ignorance. I was in a neighborhood where bigotry wasn't really questioned, and where racism and prejudice just weren't seen as a big deal. I grew up experiencing racism in many forms.

When I see people today getting upset over microaggressions, I can't help but laugh because I've dealt with the real thing: outright racism, and things that were much harsher. I remember kids from my neighborhood chasing me and throwing rocks at me while calling me every name you could imagine.

I also had to face it within the walls of my own home. I'll never forget one Thanksgiving when my Great-Grandma Rose was talking about me being bullied by the kids in the neighborhood and casually said to the whole family:

"Well, it's not his fault he's a nigger."

Real racism was something I had to navigate through every single day from a very young age. That was my daily reality. In my neighborhood on Benson Street, the kids would play a game called, and I quote, "Kill The Nigger!" And guess who was the nigger every time?

I was relentlessly picked on by these kids. But it was a strange thing, because while they were my bullies, at the same time, they were also my only friends. When you're that young, you can't really leave your block, so they were the kids I would play with. I'd go out in the morning and come back home only when the streetlights came on. Going home during the day wasn't even an option. If I did come back early, my grandmother would scream at me and tell me to go back outside.

The bullying would range from them involving me in weird, twisted games to being downright cruel, and even beating me up. I remember one time, we were playing baseball, and while I was playing catcher, I "accidentally" got hit in the head with a bat. But I knew it wasn't an accident. I knew the kid swinging the bat did it on purpose.

That kid's name was Ryan Nolan. His father, Kevin, was a big baseball fan—and a giant meathead. I can still imagine the day that he found out he was having a son, and had the genius idea: "I'm going to name him Ryan. Ryan Nolan! It's the opposite of Nolan Ryan, get it?" He must have been so proud of himself. What a moron.

Ryan was a year older than me, with dirty blond hair and blue eyes. He was the kid in the neighborhood who was the most well to do. His grandmother owned much of the property on Benson Street and was my Aunt Anna Marie and Great-Grandma Rose's landlord. Ryan was the kid with the Nintendo, the pool, and all the cool toys that he relished in not sharing with me.

I have a really embarrassing memory from when I was very young. Ryan, his sister Carly, and their dad were in the pool. The pool was actually behind my aunt and grandma's house. They lived next door to the landlord, and they built a pool in a strange communal spot. I remember standing outside of the pool looking in while they swam around playing.

I was just hoping they'd invite me in. After a little while their dad got annoyed with my presence and started singing "Louie, Louie" by The Kingsman. They all laughed. Assholes.

I wasn't the only one in my family that was getting bullied. My Uncle Raymond (who was my mother's younger brother, and someone who would drift in and out of my childhood) was in great shape, constantly doing push-ups and constantly in and out of jail for petty crimes. He knew a few sleight-of-hand magic tricks that he taught me, and he always carried cool shit like nunchucks and butterfly knives. I looked up to him. He came off like a badass.

He wore a pair of black leather gloves specifically for street fighting. Said they were to protect his knuckles when he cracked someone's jaw. He told wild stories about fighting three guys at once in jail. He always reeked of weed and danger. In my mind, he was tough. He was the kind of guy nobody fucked with.

One day, I was sitting on my aunt's front porch when I saw Uncle Raymond run past. At first, I thought, "Damn, he's always training and working out." But a few seconds later, this dude Tony Pruitt came running after him. He was chasing my uncle. Tony just happened to be the uncle of my archnemesis from the neighborhood, Nick Gianelli. Nick was the worst of my bullies. And there was his uncle Tony, sprinting down the street. And there was my Uncle Raymond, running away like a pussy.

That moment did something to me. It was embarrassing, not just for me, but for him. I thought, "Damn, how humiliating must that have been, knowing your own nephew saw you run away like that?" But more than that, I saw myself in him. Someone from my tribe running scared from someone in theirs. And I knew, right then, I don't ever want to be that guy.

I will say, when it came to bullies, my mother did teach me some valuable life lessons on how to deal with them. She taught me to stand up for myself. I used to come home almost every day in tears because the kids in my neighborhood were bullying me. I guess, after a while, she got sick of hearing it.

One day, she looked at me and said:

"If you punch these little motherfuckers in the face one time, they won't bully you anymore. Even if they beat you up, they'll stop picking on you. Bullies don't want to fight; they want to bully. So, if you fight them, they'll get tired of it."

Still, I was scared. No one had ever taught me how to fight. But fighting is kind of intuitive. If you get into enough of them, your survival instinct kicks in. You learn how to move, how to avoid being hit, and how to land a punch of your own.

I was never great at it. I think I was just willing to take a hit to give one back, and that, I believe, is the difference between the kids who fight and the kids who don't. Most people are terrified of being hit. But I'd been getting hit for as long as I could remember. It just wasn't that bad. I could take it.

The real problem was that they ganged up on me. Three or four of them at once, circling me, taking cheap shots. One time, I was riding my bike down the street and one of them jammed a stick in my spokes. I flew over the handlebars and busted my ass.

When I was about nine or ten, I started taking ceramic painting classes on Friday nights. It was at a little shop on the corner of Railroad Avenue and Route 9W, right next to where my friend Mike lived (who you'll meet later). Real nerdy shit, but I always had that side in me. We'd pay for a ceramic figure, usually like three or four bucks, and the woman who owned the shop would let us use her paints and supplies. She'd give tips and help out the younger kids.

I was pretty good at it. It was something to do with my ADHD in a world before smartphones. Most of the time, I painted things for my Aunt Anna Marie and my Great-Grandma Rose. A praying Virgin Mary, Jesus on the cross, an Easter Bunny, a teddy bear, a life-sized cat sculpture that I painted to look like our cat, Miss Kitty. They didn't really have figures I was into—no Ninja Turtles, no Transformers—so I just painted gifts for the family. My aunt still has some of them to this day.

One time, I saw they had cow skulls, ceramic ones in different sizes. I thought they looked badass. I paid four dollars for a smaller one and painted it completely white. It was already white. That's how the unpainted ceramics came. But I added a coat of white paint anyway. I didn't know what else to do with it, so I just called it done, and started walking home to Benson Street.

A few houses before mine, I saw a group of my bullies hanging out: Nick Gianelli, the oldest and the worst of the bunch; JR Robinson, who was a year older than me; his little brother Tommy, who was younger; and Ryan Nolan. They saw the skull in my hands and came running.

"Let me see that," Ryan said.

"No way," I snapped, gripping it tighter. I knew they were looking for trouble.

Nick stepped forward. "We're not going to ask again." Nick was my sister's age, and a few inches taller than me. He was lanky but strong looking. He had blond hair and blue eyes. Hitler would have loved him. He was an intimidating kid on his own.

He wasn't on his own though. I was surrounded. I didn't want to get jumped, so I handed it over. But I made one last attempt at saving it.

"Please be careful," I said. "It's the last thing my father gave me before he died."

Nick looked at me. "Really?"

"Yes," I said. "It's the only thing I have from him."

He nodded, and then hurled the skull as hard as he could down the block. I heard it explode into dust. My eyes welled up. It didn't matter that the story was a lie. I was furious. Because to them, it was real. They thought they were destroying the last connection I had to my dead father. That was their intent. That was enough.

I screamed, "Fuck you!"

They all laughed. Nick got in my face. "Get the fuck out of here before I kick your ass."

I was pissed, but I wasn't stupid. I knew I wasn't winning a fight if they all ganged up on me. So, I ran home, crying. When I got inside, my mother asked what happened. I told her about the ceramic skull. Not the lie, just that they had broken it.

She said, "Fuck this. Get your sneakers back on."

She walked me up the street to JR's house, where they had been hanging out. Only JR and Tommy were there. She lit into them.

"You little motherfuckers want to pick on him when there's four of you? You don't have the balls to fight one-on-one."

She sounded like a fight promoter, hyping up a match.

JR, trying to save face, said his little brother could take me. Tommy, smaller than me and honestly not one of the worst of the bunch, reluctantly stepped up. We squared off. I threw a wild haymaker with my eyes half-closed and clocked him right in the nose. Blood poured out. He cried and ran inside. JR just rolled his eyes.

Then it was JR's turn. He tried to tackle me. We wrestled standing up until we broke apart. Same thing. I threw a blind punch and caught him clean on the side of the face. He stepped back, red-faced, and asked, "Have you had enough?"

He wanted out. We both knew it. The fight was over.

Next stop: Ryan Nolan's house. My mom knocked on the door and gave the same Don King speech. She was in full promoter mode. I was starting to feel good. Confident. I didn't realize I could actually hurt people, and JR and Tommy were easy work.

Ryan came outside, and we started going at it. Grabbing collars, swinging wildly. We tumbled onto the hood of a parked car. I ended up on top, but he was holding my wrists. I couldn't land a punch, so I grabbed both sides of his head and started slamming it into the hood of the car, over and over.

My mom was in the background, cheering me on like I was her little Puerto Rican Rocky. He finally gave up and ran inside, teary-eyed. That made me 3–0 in official competition, and I felt unstoppable. By now, a small crowd had formed. A few adults from the neighborhood were out watching, hootin' and hollerin'. And standing there among them was Nick, the same Nick who shattered my ceramic skull.

I marched right up to him, "Not so tough when you're alone, huh?"

I shoved him in the chest. I was amped up. I felt invincible. "Let's go, you pussy!"

Nick stepped back, then cocked his fist and hit me square in the nose. Hard. Harder than I'd ever been hit in my life. Everything went blurry after that. I don't remember much, just that I didn't land a single shot, and he didn't miss one. At some point, he had me on the ground, and I was screaming:

"Mom! Help! Shit! Help me!" Eventually, she pulled him off me.

I walked away with two black eyes and a busted lip. But she was right. After that day, those kids stopped fucking with me. Turns out, even bullies don't want to deal with the crazy little Puerto Rican kid avenging his father's death, and the even crazier bitch of a mother who was promoting his fights.

As I mentioned earlier, my grandma was incredibly mean—though not to my sister, who was two years older than me and presented as White, whereas I clearly looked Puerto Rican. We shared a similar appearance, but she was very pale and fair skinned. My grandma never seemed to have much patience for kids in general, but especially for me.

I remember playing games like *Monopoly* or *The Game of Life* with my sister, and while kids that age should be laughing and enjoying themselves, every time we'd start to have fun, my grandma would scream from the back bedroom:

"Shut up! Stop carrying on! Stop it, you little motherfuckers!"

It was as if she was determined to kill any joy or laughter we had. It was psychotic, honestly. To suppress the natural happiness that kids are supposed to feel was crazy to me. I already had a father who was dead and a mother who was addicted to drugs. You'd think that'd be enough for anyone to deal with at such a young age. The woman was just so unnecessarily cruel.

I try not to hold resentment toward my Great-Grandma Rose. And as I reflect on her behavior now, I try to make an effort to view it with more empathy. By the time we were living with her, she was very physically ill and dealt with a lot of pain from having osteoporosis.

Still, growing up in that environment taught me something valuable: That when I became a father, I knew that practicing peaceful parenting was essential. I now understand how crucial it is for my child to experience the joy of life and all the small, formative moments that shape someone into a well-rounded individual.

Looking back, I feel like my sister and I were robbed of much of that.

## CHAPTER 3

# SIT BACK DOWN

Needless to say, my father's death, my mother's addiction, and being bullied every day wasn't helpful to my academic performance. By second grade, I was already struggling at school. I craved attention and became the class clown, making jokes and doing anything to avoid doing my work. I had severe ADHD, though it wasn't recognized at the time. I wasn't diagnosed until my thirties when I finally saw a psychiatrist.

As a kid, no one ever really took the time to understand what I was going through. There was no school psychologist, no teacher who thought, "Let's help this kid before he becomes a problem." But by that point, I had already become a problem. I was just the "bad kid" in second grade—unable to sit still, constantly drawing on my arms with markers, making paper airplanes, and throwing them at teachers. Getting attention for being funny was the only positive attention I could get.

But school, in general, was incredibly hard for me. In third grade, I had Miss Burrows, a pretty mean, crabby lady—one of those teachers who'd been around for decades and was just counting down the days until retirement. She was more interested in the next cigarette break than actually teaching. We had about thirty-five kids in the class, and we were all expected to learn in a very specific way.

If you couldn't fit into that mold, you were out of luck. Thankfully, things are different today. If I were a student now, and someone saw that I was acing standardized tests, had a high IQ, and was deeply committed to the work I was passionate about, like art and writing, they'd create a program tailored to my needs. They'd likely put me in a special education program that made sense for me, one where I could have truly thrived.

But that didn't happen back then. I feel like the school system failed me as a kid, and honestly, I know I'm not the only one. A lot of kids who later learned they had undiagnosed ADHD were also let down by a system that just didn't know how to help.

My school had a tiered system of education. There were the higher-level classes for the "smart" kids, mostly White. Then there were the middle-tier students, a more mixed group, and at the bottom, there was the low-level class, which, as you might guess, was primarily made up of Black and Puerto Rican kids.

These were often the kids who struggled to pay attention, caused trouble, or sometimes both. It was a form of segregation, and honestly, it was a terrible way to try to teach children. It wasn't just ineffective; it was wrong.

By fourth grade, I was already in the low-level class and got a teacher named Miss Woska. For the first time, I thought a teacher was genuinely cool. She had a great energy about her, and she inspired me. In her class, I started doing well, and for the first time, I actually looked forward to going to school and doing the work.

I remember receiving positive feedback from her, and it felt amazing. Being told I was smart for the first time really meant something to me. All it took was a teacher who was even a little bit understanding to make a huge difference.

I remember one spring, about three-quarters through the school year, Miss Woska brought her daughter to class for something like a "bring your kid to work" day. Her daughter was older, maybe seventeen or eighteen, college-aged. I can still picture it: Miss Woska had all the kids sitting on the floor, and then she said:

"Okay, I want you to stand up if you think you're one of my best students."

About six or seven kids stood up, including me, because I felt proud of my work and thought I was doing well. But then Miss Woska pointed at me and said:

"Oh, Luis, what are you doing? Sit back down."

I sat down, trying to laugh it off and act like it didn't bother me, but it really did. That moment stuck with me. Looking back, I think it was a turning point in my life. If Miss Woska had handled it with more empathy, with just a little kindness, it could have made a huge difference.

Maybe it would've set me on a different path. Not that I'm complaining about how my life turned out, I'm truly blessed and wouldn't change a thing. But in that moment,

I was once again denied basic compassion from someone I looked up to, someone who, as a teacher, should have been a source of inspiration.

The word inspiration is a meaningful one. Inspiration was one thing that was never a part of life's equation living on Benson Street. Most of the kids I grew up with had messed up childhoods. The reality is, these kids were raised by the same struggling, poor parents who dealt with substance issues, bigotry, and abuse. Parents who had been through the same things as their own parents. It was a cycle.

And in the neighborhood where I lived, there was no real motivation to break out of that cycle. No inspiration to rise above what your parents had experienced. No one was striving to do better, to win at life, or to change the world.

No one was trying. When I moved to New York City at nineteen, which we'll get into later in the book, everyone around me was driven. People were striving to do their best, to get ahead, and to lead. It was inspiring. The energy, the attitude, the ambition. Everyone there had a goal.

Everyone was trying to be the best version of whatever they were. You'd be on the subway, and you would find yourself sitting next to a guy worth $10 million that works on Wall Street sitting across from someone selling their music album, hoping to become the biggest rapper in the world.

Everyone is trying to be the best. The best musicians, dancers, and actors all come from New York. Even the homeless people seemed more motivated than in other cities. The homeless didn't just beg, they performed for you or told you an elaborate story. They were trying to be the best goddamn homeless person they could possibly be!

But where I was living in Rockland County, New York, on Benson Street, in the '80s and '90s, the mindset was completely different. No one was aiming to be the best at anything. The goal for most people in my neighborhood was simply to become something like a garbage man. A city job with reliable pay.

"Now that's a good job," I remember my aunt always saying.

That was considered an aspirational career. People's biggest dreams were as low as sifting through garbage. There's an old saying: "Shoot for the moon and you'll land among the stars."

It's supposed to inspire you to aim higher and set bigger goals. It suggests that even if you don't achieve your ultimate aim, you'll still achieve something significant.

For the people of Benson Street, it's: "Shoot for the garbage and maybe you'll land something slightly better than minimum wage."

## CHAPTER 4

# DEAD MAN'S HUSTLE

For as long as I could remember, my mother had complained about money problems. I was so acutely aware that we were poor. It was embarrassing. Embarrassing when she pulled out food stamps at the supermarket. Embarrassing to always be driving around in some beat-up car. She might as well have strapped a loudspeaker to the roof that blared:

"Hey everyone, we're poor and on welfare!"

I knew from an early age that I had to start making moves if I wanted things to change. One of my first entrepreneurial endeavors was when I was seven or eight years old. Now at this point, I was starting up iced tea stands and shoveling people's driveways, doing whatever I could do to make money.

One day, my arch nemesis, Nick Gianelli, came up to me and told me that our neighbor had died. It was a guy that lived four or five doors up from me. I didn't know who he was, besides just recognizing him as an older dude that lived in the neighborhood. And now, apparently, this older dude had passed away.

Nick told me that they're putting all of his belongings out on the curb, and that he wanted to go rummage through it and maybe take some stuff. I was always looking for a way to make a buck, so I was like:

"Why don't we bring everything over to my house and have a yard sale?"

My mom picked up a gig as a receptionist at Blauvelt Windows and Doors, and essentially would just leave me with my older sister home alone all day. At this point we had moved into an apartment next door to my aunt and grandma. We were at 54 Benson Street; they were at 52 Benson Street. Our great-grandma was supposed to be "watching" us, but never really did. So, now I had my entire front yard available to sell this dead guy's shit from.

So, me and Nick started moving over all of the belongings they were putting out for trash. There was a leather love seat, a lazy boy, some tables and chairs, a dining room set, a TV, and a dart board. Basically, it was a lot of shit you'd see contestants bidding on in a game of *The Price is Right.* There was also a poster of four chicks in bikinis, which I ended up keeping for myself and putting on my bedroom wall.

After we moved all of the stuff over to my yard, we started labeling things. We labeled the leather love seat for like six bucks, the lazy boy for three dollars, and the dart board for twenty-five cents. We were kids and had no sense of what these items should cost. When we were labeling everything, we were thinking:

"Six bucks for a love seat? Nobody's ever going to pay that much money. That's crazy."

And of course, a few hours later, we sold out of everything. There was nothing left.

Word quickly got around town about this yard sale with vastly underpriced goods, and they just flocked right to it. There was a line of people waiting to come into my yard to grab all of this older dead guy's belongings. I ended up making, I want to say, fifty or sixty bucks for the day.

I think that experience helped shaped who I am to this very day. Had I not been successful, maybe I never would have become an entrepreneur. But luckily, it turned out to be a huge success.

I also have to give some credit to that kid Nick, the worst of all my bullies. If he hadn't told me about that old man dying and his stuff being tossed out, I might not have become the person I am today. He was a total piece of shit, and I couldn't stand him back then, but looking back, I can still appreciate the role he played in my life. That one random interaction ended up being a defining moment for me. It planted the seed to hustle, earn, and make my own money.

Things weren't always so smooth during my formative entrepreneurial days. One time, when I was about ten years old, I went door to door asking if anyone needed any odd jobs done. I'd do whatever: clean out a garage, mow a lawn, paint a fence. I wasn't particularly good at any of these jobs, but I really wanted money. Having cash felt great, and watching my mother struggle financially messed with my head.

One hot summer day, I knocked on a door about ten houses away from my own. A young dude answered. At the time, he seemed like an adult, but thinking back, he was probably eighteen or nineteen years old. He was shirtless and reeked of beer and weed.

I gave him my pitch: "Hey, I live in the neighborhood, and I was wondering if you needed any chores or odd jobs done around the house!" I smiled. You have to smile in sales. It's contagious.

The guy, who seemed friendly enough, said, "Actually, I could use help cleaning up behind my shed."

He led me to the backyard. Behind the shed was a massive pile of empty beer bottles, hundreds of them. It looked like he'd been sneaking back there to drink and just dumping them. He probably didn't want his parents to find out.

He said, "Clean up all these bottles, and I'll give you ten bucks."

Ten dollars to a ten-year-old in 1992 was like a thousand dollars today. I could buy candy, hit the arcade, and still have money left for a rainy day. Hell yes! I took the job.

It only took me about an hour to bag everything up, but it was hot as hell, and my hands were sticky from spilled beer. When I finished, I went back to his door and knocked.

"Hey, mister, I'm all done."

He looked me over and said, "Thanks. Now get the fuck out of here."

"What about my ten dollars?" I asked.

He laughed. "I was never going to give you ten dollars, you idiot."

I felt my head start to burn. "You promised me ten bucks if I cleaned up those bottles. Now pay me!"

He snapped, "I said get the fuck out of here, you little shit," and slammed the door in my face.

I was so fucking pissed! This was insane! We had a deal! This was the purest definition of the word unethical. I couldn't and wouldn't let it slide.

I stormed back to the backyard. The proof of my work was there, three large trash bags full of empty bottles, tied up and sitting against the shed. I grabbed one and dragged it behind the shed. Then I started taking bottles out, one by one, and smashing them on the ground.

"Rip me off?" Smash.

"Fucking asshole." Smash.

"I'll show you." Smash.

After smashing nearly every bottle in the first bag, I heard the back door swing open and slam shut. I peeked around the shed and saw the guy, still shirtless, and now furious, charging at me.

I ran through the glass and tried to hop the fence into the next yard, but he caught me by the collar just before I could get over. He dragged me by the shirt straight through the shards of broken glass. My legs and hands got shredded.

"You're going to clean this up again," he growled, "Or I'm going to beat the shit out of you."

So, I did. I cleaned the shit up. Again.

I went home and told my mother, expecting her to do something. She said she was going to go to his house, but she never did.

# CHAPTER 5

# YOU DON'T RAT

As I was starting to get a little older and getting into the fifth and sixth grades, I started becoming friends with more Hispanic and Black kids. Kids who looked like me. I would venture off Benson Street. I was becoming more independent. One of those kids was Mike Guerrier. Mike lived up on the corner of Route 9W and Railroad Avenue, which was maybe a ten-minute walk from where I lived on Benson Street. Mike was a dark-skinned Dominican, and had a big afro that he would sometimes braid. Mike and I became best friends.

He was a good dude. He also had an older brother named Sergio who was two or three years older than us. And I liked Sergio as well. Me and Mike would hang out almost daily and Sergio was there sometimes too. Sergio and Mike also came from a poor household. Their mom was also using food stamps and was on Section 8.

They were in a similar situation. Rarely did we have extra money for things that we wanted. To make some cash for video games and candy, we decided to start breaking into cars in the Grand Union and ShopRite parking lots.

When I say, "breaking in," we weren't smashing windows or anything, we would just simply go around the parking lot, look for doors that were open, and then clear out all of the change in the center console.

And this was the early '90s, so everyone had at least a handful of change in their center console. That was our jackpot.

So, this is how we would pay for things like candy, movies, and video games. A little bit of cash back then, for a couple kids like us, went a long way. I'd say on a good day we would score four or five bucks, and after a while we got pretty used to stealing. It became a routine.

One time, Mike and I opened up a door to a pickup truck parked outside a store and there was a brown paper bag on the front seat which we quickly snatched and ran off with. In the bag was a bottle of liquor—which we threw away, but also in the bag was $200. Two one-hundred-dollar bills. This was a huge score for us.

When we told Mike's older brother Sergio about the score, he said to us, "I'll give you guys twenty dollars each and I'm taking the rest of the money." He wasn't even there. He literally took $160 away from us and walked away like it was nothing. There's nothing we could do. Sergio was bigger than us.

At this point, I kind of had a Venn diagram of friends. I was hanging out with Mike and Sergio, and some of the kids from Railroad Ave., which was a rough block. I ended up moving to Railroad Ave. in the summer between the sixth and seventh grades. It was mostly Hispanic and Black kids who I fit in with as opposed to the White kids who hated me on Benson Street. I would go to Mike's house and play video games, and his mom would cook us Dominican food. I became pretty close with him and his family.

Then there was the aforementioned asshole, Ryan Nolan. Mike and Sergio had early insight into Ryan. They instinctively knew he sucked. They knew he was also kind of a pussy. Just a little bitch. Mike and Sergio didn't care much for Ryan. They didn't really interact with him a lot, but they sort of knew him, and they knew that his family had, what we considered at the time, a lot of money. They didn't actually have a lot of money. We just knew they had more money than we had.

One time, Sergio and another kid from the neighborhood, this kid named Chris, went and they broke into Ryan's father's car. He had a green Jeep Grand Cherokee, and he had a car phone. This was before most people had car phones. They were expensive and rare. So, Sergio and Chris break into the car, steal the phone, and key the Jeep Grand Cherokee, leaving a shit ton of scratch marks on it. Then they slashed the tires as well, which, honestly, good for them. Fuck the Nolan's.

The next day after this went down, Mike called me and said:

"Yo, last night my brother and Chris robbed Ryan's dad's car phone and keyed the car."

Mike didn't even think twice about telling me something like that. He was my boy, and we were used to stealing things together. To him, sharing that info was nothing. It was just part of our world.

Later that same day, somehow, I ended up hanging out with Ryan Nolan and a couple of other kids. We were just talking, and Ryan started going off about how his dad's car had been broken into the night before. I don't know why I did it, maybe I was looking for some kind of approval from those kids, trying to fit in, but without thinking, I just blurted out:

"I know who did it."

That one dumb sentence kicked off a chain reaction. The cops got involved, and pretty soon they arrested Sergio and the kid Chris. But Chris was White and had a "good dad," so he got off easy. Sergio, on the other hand, got sent to juvenile detention for, if I remember right, around two years.

I'll never forget when the police came for me. They took me up to Chris's house and started questioning me. And again, I caved. I blurted out everything I knew. Even as the words were leaving my mouth, I felt sick with guilt. I remember thinking, what the hell am I doing? But by then it was too late. I was already in it.

During the questioning, the cops had Sergio in another room, and I heard him yell out:

"What about all those cars we robbed together?"

And I just played dumb. "I don't know what he's talking about." I said, pretending like I had no idea.

After Sergio got taken away, everything changed. Mike and I stopped being friends for almost a year. His mom was furious with me, and honestly, I couldn't even blame her. In the hood, and especially in Brown communities, you just don't rat. It's an unspoken rule. You never snitch.

Looking back, it was a weird, impulsive moment where I wanted approval from the wrong people. It was a genuine mistake, and it's something that pains me to think about to this very day.

After a while Mike accepted me back as a friend. He forgave me. I was just dumb and made a mistake. His mom's anger dialed down a few notches after being very upset with me. And a year later, Sergio came home, but Mike and his mom didn't tell me he was coming home. One day, Mike invited me over to his house, I walked up the stairs, and Sergio answered the door…and then he beat the shit out of me.

He just had to get his licks in. He hit me a few times and he was like, "You don't fucking rat, you piece of shit!" And that was that. He put it aside. And Mike, his mom, and Sergio accepted me back as a friend. I will never forget the fact that they were able to forgive me for something that, to Latinos and Brown people, is an unforgivable offense.

You don't rat. And I was a rat.

# CHAPTER 6
# RAILROAD AVENUE

After a few years on Benson Street, I eventually moved to Railroad Avenue. Most people would've considered Railroad Avenue less desirable than Benson Street, but for me, it felt like a huge step up.

Our apartment on the second floor of 35 Railroad Avenue was nicer than the one at 54 Benson Street, and for the first time, I felt like I actually belonged somewhere. The kids in that neighborhood looked like me, came from the same kind of homes, and understood the kind of life I was living.

Our little crew from Railroad Avenue was made up of a bunch of scrappy kids who all thought we were tougher than we really were. Looking back now, it's almost funny. None of us were real gangsters. We were just a pack of broke kids trying to carve out some kind of identity in a town that didn't give us much to work with. At best, someone might have called us "suburban thugs," and even that probably would've been a stretch.

I got especially close with James Salcone, the only White kid in the neighborhood, who lived two doors up from me. Pauly lived right next door. On the other side were Cano and Miguel, who were Puerto Rican brothers. And then up on the corner, there were Mike and Sergio. That was our little squad. We had each other's back, no questions asked.

Every now and then, there were fights, but most of the time it was just kids throwing hands, talking trash, and puffing up their chests. You didn't hear about kids getting shot every week or bodies turning up in the street. It wasn't that kind of neighborhood. It was rough, yeah, but it wasn't deadly.

Compared to where I was born in Paterson, New Jersey, Rockland County was a step up, even in the worst parts. Paterson had real danger: hardcore violence, murders, and serious drug wars.

Rockland County, at least the side I grew up on, was more like the poor tragedy of the suburbs. It was the forgotten side. The place where broken families, food stamps, and dead-end futures lived, but it wasn't quite a war zone. We were struggling, but we weren't in constant mortal danger.

But Paterson, New Jersey, has always had a reputation for being one of the roughest places in the country. Even today, it's still considered one of the most dangerous cities in America. It's a place that's really fallen apart over the years: dilapidated buildings, abandoned lots, and open-air drug markets.

Back when I was a kid, it was already bad, but from what I hear and see now, it's only gotten worse. Paterson today is one of the heroin capitals of the world, a real epicenter of addiction, poverty, and violence. It's sad, honestly, because there's also a lot of history there, a lot of culture, but it just got swallowed up by crime, corruption, drugs, and a broken system.

There was a lot of pressure growing up. It was not just the pressure to survive but the pressure to take responsibility for my own life far earlier than most kids ever have to. It wasn't just about growing up fast, it was also about basic survival. I was stressed by it. I worried about whether we'd have cable, or a working phone, or even electricity. Worried about eviction. At eleven years old, I was carrying anxiety most adults would crack under.

Section 8 was supposed to make housing affordable. Let's say our rent was $1,300 a month. Section 8 would cover maybe $1,150 of that, and my mom would be responsible for the remaining $150 or so. And she couldn't even come up with that. It wasn't that she wasn't capable. My mom wasn't dumb, far from it. She was actually really smart. But she had this loser mentality, like life had already beaten her, so why bother trying? There was no fight left in her, no drive. No belief in herself.

That crushed me more than anything, watching her check out, just give up on herself, and by extension, on us. So, I started working, not just because I had to, but because I wanted more. I used to fantasize about money. Not just for the sake of having it, but for what it represented: safety, comfort, dignity. I wanted nice things. I wanted to walk into school and not feel ashamed of what I was wearing or whether I had supplies. I wanted to feel like a normal kid.

I remember being a little kid and feeling this strange moral discomfort about it all. I didn't have the language for it then, but I felt it. I had this little internal monologue that sounded more like a young Republican than a kid from the hood: "Why are other people's tax dollars going toward my mom sitting in her room watching TV all day?" I knew it wasn't fair to think that way, not entirely.

But when you're a kid growing up in that kind of instability, and you're the one out there trying to earn money while your parent is home watching daytime TV, those kinds of thoughts creep in. You start to wonder what's broken.

Whatever it was, I just had this awareness that the world didn't owe you anything. I knew that sitting on your ass and expecting other people to pay your bills wasn't how life was supposed to work. Something inside me rejected that, even at that young age, and I decided very early on that when I'm an adult, I will never be poor. I was going to make money, be self-sufficient, and build something for myself.

Ironically, that mindset and those values were lessons my mom taught me, just by being who she was. Not intentionally, but through contrast. Watching her laziness and her inability to grow beyond the bare minimums of life were lessons learned by witnessing them.

## CHAPTER 7

# THE JOB MARKET

By the time I was eleven years old, I was already hunting for a job. That was the year I landed my first real paying gig, and I haven't stopped working since.

My first job was selling newspaper subscriptions for *The Rockland Journal News*. There was an ad in that very same paper that said: "Earn Money P/T after school working for The Rockland Journal News!" It was technically a door-to-door job, but we weren't just knocking on people's houses, we worked parking lots.

I'd hang around outside supermarkets waiting for people to come and go, and hit them with a pitch that went something like:

"Hey, my name's Luis. I'm in a contest with *The Rockland Journal News*; we're giving away free newspaper subscriptions. If you sign up for eight weeks, totally free, you can cancel anytime. The more people I get to sign up, the better my chances I have of winning a free bike!"

That was a lie.

In reality, there was no contest and no bike. I got paid five dollars for every household that I signed up for a free subscription. The newspaper was banking on the fact that most people just forget to cancel after eight weeks. The whole operation was run by some shady random guy in a van. Seriously, just a guy with a van full of eleven- and twelve-year-old kids, driving us around to different neighborhoods to hustle subscriptions.

Looking back, it sounds like the beginning of a Netflix true-crime documentary. But at the time, nobody seemed to think much of it. All our parents just let this guy pick us up and take us wherever. No background checks. No questions. Just a "be home by dinner."

It turns out I was really good at it. Like, really good. I was pulling in $300 to $400 a week, which, at the time, was twice as much as my mom was making. I didn't even fully grasp how crazy that was. I just knew I had a knack for talking to people and instantly reading them. Figuring out how to get them to say yes. That job lasted about two months, maybe a little more, before things fell apart. The guy running the operation started bouncing checks.

My mom found out I wasn't getting paid for everything I was owed, and that was the end of that. She made me quit. Still, that job left a mark on me. I'll never forget this one afternoon, we were knocking on doors in a predominantly Orthodox Jewish neighborhood. It was me and another kid, a Black kid, and we knocked on this woman's door. She peeked through the curtain and said:

"Hold on."

So, we waited. A couple of minutes passed. We rang the doorbell again. She popped back into the window:

"Hold on, I'll be right there."

So, we kept waiting, figuring she was grabbing her wallet or something. Next thing we know, two cop cars pull up and block us in. The bitch had called the police on us. We were just standing there, doing our job, and she apparently saw two kids she didn't trust.

That moment stuck with me. It showed me how people perceive you before you even say a word. We weren't doing anything wrong, but that didn't matter.

Despite everything, that job taught me a lot. It taught me how to stop a stranger in their tracks and get them to listen. It taught me how to turn a "no" into a "yes." It was my first real experience with sales, with understanding body language, tone, and timing. That experience was invaluable for me. Most people can't do sales and I learned very early on that I could do sales.

Years later, I answered another ad, this time in *The Village Voice*. That one led me to a job selling tickets for the New York Comedy Club, which we'll get to later on.

By the time I was eleven, I had already pretty much realized that if I wanted anything like new clothes, a toy, something for school, I was going to have to figure out how to get it myself. That was just the reality.

My mom had stopped buying me school clothes around then, and not long after that, she stopped buying us Christmas gifts. I think at that point, she decided her job as a parent was done. She was basically on her own at twelve years old. She was already raising her four little brothers. In her eyes, once you hit twelve you were basically an adult and on your own. It's crazy.

Eventually, my mom did pick up a job at a hair salon, which became my second job too. She worked as a shampoo girl. She had actually gone to cosmetology school and finished the coursework. She could have been a really good hairdresser. She was artistic and had a passion for it. But passion wasn't the problem. The problem was the follow-through.

She never took the final licensing exam. She did all the work, put in the hours, and then just stopped short. I could never understand that. Like, why go through all that schooling, all that effort, and then not take the last step? If she had, she could've worked as a licensed stylist instead of washing other people's hair for tips.

The place she started working at was a high-end beauty salon in New City, New York, called Bruno's. It was a pretty rich neighborhood made up of mostly White and Jewish families, a world apart from Railroad Avenue.

The owner was this obviously gay man, and his wife was this big Colombian woman. At the time, they seemed really rich to me. They had a big house and drove a Mercedes-Benz. I went to their house once. They hired me to paint their pool. Now that I think back on it, maybe they weren't as rich as I remembered. Hiring an eleven-year-old to paint your pool doesn't seem like a rich person move. It was also a job I was totally unable to do. I never finished the job and the section that I painted looked like shit. You get what you pay for.

Anyway, my mom was just a shampoo girl at the salon. And the thing is, there was a path for her to move up. She could've become a hairdresser, maybe even a colorist. There's

good money in that line of work. Over time, you build up a loyal client base, sharpen your craft, and if you're smart with your money, maybe you even save enough to open your own place. You make a plan, follow the steps, and eventually, you're not just an employee, you're a business owner. An entrepreneur. That's always how I've seen things. I've always been able to connect the dots. A leads to B, B leads to C. You lay the groundwork, set the table, and eventually you start to reap the rewards.

But my mom never saw things that way. She couldn look past what was right in front of her. Some people are ju wired differently. You can't reprogram that. And I've come t understand that I'm lucky, blessed even, to have this inn drive and belief in myself. That instinct to survive, to hust to figure things out. If you dropped me in the middle of t woods with nothing, I'd still become me. I'd be the guy w figured it out. I'd find a way to lead, to make something o of nothing. My mom didn't have that. She just didn't h that gear.

So, I ended up working at the salon when I was ele years old. One day a week, on Saturdays. My main job to sweep up the hair off the salon floor. But I also ha side hustle of taking lunch orders from all the women worked there.

The hairdressers, the manicurists, and the colorists w all hand me their orders and I'd head over to the shop center next door to grab their food. I was doing Doorl before DoorDash was a thing. That plaza had everythi really good pizzeria, a Chinese takeout place, a sushi sp Kenny Rogers chicken place, and a Burger King. Every

was within walking distance, so I'd spend the lunch rush running back and forth with everyone's orders. They'd each tip me a buck or two, and by the time I was done, I'd usually have made about thirty or forty dollars just from that.

On Saturdays, my mom would work until about 5:00 p.m., but I'd usually finish up after lunch around 2:30. That's when I'd take the money I earned and go straight to Knick Knacks 2, a gift shop owned by the dad of a girl I went to school with. It had a pretty solid selection of magic tricks, pranks, and gags. I'd spend every Saturday treating myself: I'd buy a movie ticket, sit in the theater alone with a popcorn and a soda, and just enjoy some quiet time. After the movie, I'd spend another ten to twenty bucks on a new magic trick.

That became a little ritual for me. I got really into sleight-of-hand magic and started building up a collection of tricks. Magic tricks have always been something I had an interest in. And even now, all these years later, it's something that I still do with my son.

Another job I had was working with my Great Uncle Howard on the weekends, delivering newspapers out of his shitty Oldsmobile. Around 2:00 a.m., we'd head to *The Rockland Journal News* building, to the actual presses, and we'd assemble the papers ourselves. We'd fold them, stuff them into plastic bags, and get them ready for delivery. My hands would always end up just covered in ink, and for some reason, the smell of whatever chemical was in those plastic bags made me want to puke every single time.

Once we had everything packed, we'd drive around the neighborhood, tossing newspapers out the car window onto people's porches. There was something kind of fun about it,

cruising around in the dead of night and launching papers at people's houses. I would pretend we were soldiers on a mission. That the papers were grenades. And I got very good at hitting the mark. The job only lasted from about 2:00 to 6:00 a.m. on weekends.

Uncle Howard was a character. Almost every job he'd ever had involved driving. He was a cab driver, a delivery guy, a truck driver, and a newspaper delivery man. He was always behind the wheel.

But one day, while driving over either the Tappan Zee or the George Washington Bridge, someone robbed his cab and bashed his skull in with a hammer. It nearly killed him. After that, he was never quite the same. He had this deep indentation in his skull, where you could literally fit a couple fingers into it. Oddly enough, that made him kind of a hit at parties.

All of these jobs, from selling newspaper subscriptions, sweeping up hair at the salon, fetching lunches, and delivering newspapers, happened within the same year. That was the year I discovered "the hustle." It was also the year I discovered...puberty.

# CHAPTER 8
# THE PUBE

It's safe to say that when puberty hit, I was much more than the average horny little boy. Bruno's, the salon that I worked in, was loaded with all smoking hot chicks. Every girl working at the salon was a smoking hot twenty-one-year-old hairdresser, and I was in absolute fucking heaven. Every single one of them was gorgeous, strutting around in tight clothes: miniskirts, low-cut tops, the works. By halfway through the day, I couldn't take it anymore. I'd sneak down to the basement, jerk my little dick, then stroll back upstairs like nothing happened. Business as usual, you know?

There was this one girl I was obsessed with. Her name was Eileen. She was a shampoo girl like my mom, but twenty-one years old, half-Asian, and super fucking hot. One day, she walked out of the bathroom, and I slipped in right after her. I spotted a pube on the toilet seat. So, I did what any eleven-year-old, red blooded American boy would do: I picked it up, put it in my mouth, and jerked off.

After I was done, I saved the pube for future use. Looking back, though, I've got no clue if it was actually Eileen's. She was just the last one in there. Could have been anyone's pube, really. Hell, it could have been a guy's. Could have been my mom's! Guess we'll never know. Fate's a tricky, unpredictable bitch.

I definitely had an overactive libido for my age. I've always wondered if catching my mom with that guy Tom when I was younger fucked me up a bit, subconsciously. Who knows?

My mom didn't put any limits on what movies I could watch, either. Back then, it wasn't uncommon for kids to see R-rated flicks, but my mom took it to a whole other level. We didn't just watch horror or action movies. We watched some seriously fucked up shit.

I watched *The Accused* with her, which has that brutal gang rape scene. I was maybe seven when we watched *A Clockwork Orange* together—a movie that's fucked up on every level.

There's this one scene in *A Clockwork Orange* that's seared into my brain. The main characters are in a gang, and they invade a couple's safe, countryside home. They cut the nipples out of the woman's red jumpsuit, tie up her husband—an older guy in a wheelchair—and rape her right in front of him. Holding his face and forcing him watch. It's a huge plot point, and even now, it's disturbing as hell. I was seven years old watching this shit.

I remember this dark, heavy feeling washing over me. A sick knot in the pit of my stomach. I was learning what rape was, and my mom was just sitting there, watching the movie, not thinking about how this might fuck me up later or, at the very least, give me some weird kinks.

In 1993, I was eleven. It was a different time. Nobody had the internet yet. You couldn't just pull out an iPhone and find a million porn videos to jerk off to. You kids today have no idea how good you've got it. Back then, we had the *Playboy Channel*—channel 99. We didn't have a subscription, but if you flipped up or down to a channel, and timed it just right, you'd maybe get half a second of a clear picture. Tilt your head sideways, and sometimes you could make out a nipple. And you know what? That was enough.

Around this time, I discovered masturbating. And holy shit, I'd jerk off to everything. I'd plop down in front of the TV, flip through channels, and get myself off to whatever woman was on the screen at that moment. That was my game. I had to just jerk off to whoever was on TV right then and there. It was this weird little addiction. I craved variety. Couldn't get enough of it.

Throughout the years, I would start building a solid collection of porn magazines. I'd flip through them, but after a few sessions, I'd get bored with the girls. The last few pages of those mags always had ads for 800 and 900 numbers, and yeah, I'd jerk off to the girls in those ads too. I was insatiable! Always chasing that variety.

When I was eleven, my mom straight up bought me a dirty magazine: an issue of *Gallery*. I think she was trying to be this open-minded, progressive mom, creating an atmosphere where sexuality wasn't some taboo thing. Hell, maybe she was just way ahead of her time with feminism and sex work.

Nowadays, girls doing sex work wear it like a badge of honor. Everyone knows someone with an OnlyFans. It just isn't that big of a deal. There's less shame now than there used to be. Back then, nobody really thought of sex workers like that, but that was mom's mentality. Thank God for it.

She must have known I was in my bedroom jerking off all the time. So, one day, she was like, "Alright, I'll buy you a dirty magazine."

We went to this little newsstand with a rack of adult mags. I didn't want to pick anything too graphic in front of my mom, so I grabbed *Gallery*, which had this gorgeous brunette on the cover with icy blue eyes. Dark hair, light eyes? She must have been a wild one.

*Gallery* ended up becoming a hardcore mag, later. But back then, it was just pages of beautiful, naked women. Nothing too graphic. No spread eagle shots or anything. It was like *Playboy* without the articles, just the centerfolds. That magazine was my first true love, man. We went to hell and back together. It stayed with me for a long time.

What my mom didn't know was that I already had a *Hustler* magazine I found in the woods months earlier. I kept it hidden in my room, stashed in the drop ceiling above my bed. I'd move the ceiling panel and tuck it up there like it was my secret treasure.

I remember this one time I was hanging with my sister's friend, Surelis. She was a few years older than me, maybe thirteen, and I was eleven. We were in the woods near my house, flipping through that *Hustler* magazine together. Just the two of us. She started getting turned on and said something like, "I'm so horny. Wouldn't it be cool if we fucked?"

I just let out this loud, cartoonish gulp and acted like I didn't hear her. I regretted passing up that opportunity for *most of my teenage years.* Thinking about it now it's pretty fucked up. For a girl that young to say something like that, God knows what kind of upbringing she had. She might have been molested or something, which could've made her a total mental mess.

If I'd taken her up on it that day in the woods, it probably would've just been another bad memory for her to unpack with some therapist later on.

By the time I was heading into high school, the internet was just starting to become a thing. I think it was around seventh or eighth grade when a lot of people started getting AOL accounts, but I didn't get mine until ninth grade. I was always a bit behind the curve when it came to technology. That was a pattern for me growing up. When everyone else was playing the latest Nintendo, I was still stuck with Atari. When the Super Nintendo came out, I still had the original Nintendo. Always one generation behind.

Around 1995 or 1996, AOL was rolling out dial-up internet. Back then, you'd get these CDs that gave you limited hours: twenty, forty, maybe sixty hours of access. You'd plug in your modem, listen to that screeching dial-up sound as it connected, and finally get online. But since it used the phone line, if someone in the house picked up the phone, your connection would drop, and you'd end up in a screaming match. That was just the new norm for my generation, and let me tell you, it set us up to be total fucking porn addicts.

We went from an era of scrambled TV screens, dirty magazines, and the occasional VHS tape passed around between friends, to suddenly having access to *everything* online. In the very beginning, you'd wait hours just to download a single picture. Streaming videos in decent quality? Forget about it. That was basically science fiction. But things evolved fast.

It went from waiting hours for one grainy image to load to having streaming sites with every category of porn you can imagine. I mean, we're at a point now where you can literally watch chicks you went to high school with starring in porn flicks. It's surreal, and honestly kind of awesome.

It was like technology and culture collided to create this new sexual revolution. For me, the timing was either perfect or tragic. Maybe both.

They just dropped porn on us. We were already drowning in puberty, hormones going wild, and then they were like, "Here, let's make an entire generation of dudes into porn addicts."

I think we got dealt a shitty hand. A hand covered in lotion, with bits of tissue stuck to it.

## CHAPTER 9

# CLUCK CLUCK

I found out that my mother had cancer when I was in the sixth grade. I remember seeing my sister after a school assembly and she was crying and I didn't know why. She was in eighth grade at the time, and we both went to the same middle school.

When we got home, she told me our mother had cancer. My mom had smoked two packs of Marlboro Reds a day for as long as I can remember. After a few bouts with chronic bronchitis, she went to the doctor and was diagnosed with throat cancer. I remember not feeling very emotional at the time. Maybe I was blocking it out or maybe it was a defense mechanism. I'm not sure.

I cared, but for some reason, I didn't get emotional. I just never felt like she was going to die. My mom was tough, and it just didn't hit me the same way it hit my sister, who was very emotional and upset. A lot of that time is a blur. Over the next few years, my mom started going to New York

Presbyterian Hospital in the city, to the ENT (Ear, Nose, and Throat) department, for radiation treatment.

Eventually, the radiation destroyed her vocal cords. By the time I was in eighth grade up until I stopped speaking to her, my mom could no longer talk. She could only whisper. She would yell and curse at me in whispers. And I know it was incredibly frustrating for her, but it was also kind of hilarious in a dark way. How can you take someone seriously when they are whisper-yelling at you?

Even though my mother was pretty attractive and thin, she did not eat very healthy. Most of her diet consisted of KFC and chocolate-covered cheesecake from ShopRite. She loved that cheesecake so much and would never share it with us. She also loved to get Pillsbury cinnamon rolls. They would come eight in a tin, and she would make them and cover five of them with all of the icing that they came with. She would let my sister and I have the remaining three but with no icing. My sister and I would fight over who got to scrape the icing scraps out of the little plastic container they came in.

My sister was painfully shy. I remember my mother bringing her with her through the KFC drive thru and my sister refused to order for her. Since my mom could only whisper, the person taking the order would think she was messing with them. It was frustrating, but again, it was kind of darkly funny too.

This scenario gave us an opportunity to fuck with my mother. Even though she was abusive, my sister and I still would jump at the opportunity to fuck with her. It was our way to get retribution.

One time, we convinced my mother that KFC was sponsoring a contest. If you drove up to the drive thru and clucked like a chicken and said, "I want some chicken," while doing your best impression of what a chicken would sound like, they would give you a free value meal.

We told her that only adults could do it so she would have to. My mother wasn't about to miss the opportunity to get some free KFC. So, with my sister in the passenger seat, and me in the back, she went through the drive thru. The teenager working said:

"Hi, welcome to KFC. Can I take your order?"

And my mom whispered, "*Cluck cluck*, can I have some chicken?"

"I'm sorry?" the teenager said.

"*Cluck cluck*, can I have some chicken?"

"Sir, I cannot understand what you're saying."

My mom was growing frustrated. "CLUCK CLUCK, can I have some fucking chicken?!"

The drive thru worker got the manager. The entire time my sister and I were howling with laughter. My mother was too busy angrily whisper-clucking to notice us. To this day, that might be the hardest I have ever laughed.

My sister, Jeneice, or, as everyone called her, Jeni, was actually really funny. I looked up to my sister a lot and her influence has shaped who I am to this very day. When we were kids, my sister would say she wanted to be a standup comedian. We would watch *Def Jam*, *Martin Lawrence*, and *Eddie Murphy* specials together.

We always connected with urban comedy. We never watched *Jerry Seinfeld* or *George Carlin*. We connected with

Black comedians talking about growing up poor, being on welfare, and dealing with abuse. That spoke to us. That's something we could understand.

My sister also was "podcasting" long before podcasting was a thing. She had a friend in elementary school named Douglas Bailey. When she was in the fifth grade, her friend Doug moved away. In reality, he just moved to New Jersey, maybe an hour away from Rockland County, but an hour for a ten-year-old might as well have been across the Atlantic. Jeni and Doug would record shows on cassette tapes and send them to each other.

My sister's show was *The Jeni Poo Show* and I was her co-host/punching bag. I'd like to think that I was the *Artie Lange* to her *Howard Stern*, but I was probably more like a *Beetlejuice* or *Stuttering John*.

Jeni used to record these shows on our answering machine, and she got really creative with them. She would pretend to interview rock stars by holding the answering machine up to the TV and recording their responses from real interviews she had taped off MTV. It took a lot of time and effort to pull off.

She would also do segments and sketches. One time, she had a "Christmas Special," where she interviewed Frosty the Snowman, Rudolph the Red-Nosed Reindeer, and Santa Claus all in one show. I wish I had her guest booker today. In reality, I played the parts of all three characters. The sketch ended with Frosty complaining about how hot the studio lights were. He melted, Rudolph tripped and fell nose-first into the puddle that Frosty made which then electrocuted Santa Claus. We killed Santa Claus on the show. I was eight.

Speaking of Christmas, there is a particular holiday memory I'd like to share: It was Christmas Eve, 1994. I remember it vividly, not just because of the holiday, but because *Street Fighter: The Movie* had just come out the day before, on December 23.

As a twelve-year-old kid, that movie was a big deal, even though it wasn't exactly a masterpiece of cinema. Every kid my age played Street Fighter 2 obsessively. I was pretty good at the game. I would play as the character Chun Li who not only was fun to play as, but she was also pretty hot. If you timed it right, you could pause the game while she did a back flip and see her ass up her skirt.

My mom took me to see the movie. Just the two of us.

I remember sitting in the theater, eating popcorn, feeling like things were okay...normal, even. We also went Christmas shopping that day, stopping at stores like Sam Goody, Circuit City, and Radio Shack. Stores that don't even exist today. It felt festive. At the time, I had no idea it would be the last Christmas where my mom would buy me and my sister gifts.

The cancer diagnosis had changed everything. She stopped working soon after, and our financial situation took a serious hit. The energy in the house shifted; everything became a little more fragile, a little more uncertain. That final "normal Christmas," she gave me a five-disc CD player, which was a big expensive gift. Along with it, she gave me two hip-hop CDs: *Onyx* and *Salt-N-Pepa*. That's right. I only had two discs for my five-disc CD player. Still, I was pumped about the gift.

I was just starting to really get into hip-hop and beginning to explore the Puerto Rican side of my identity, trying to figure out who I was in the world. Most of my friends listened to hip-hop and I was trying to fit in.

My mom drove this beat-up old Ford Mercury Topaz. The thing was loud, unreliable, and constantly on the verge of falling apart, but it got us where we needed to go. After our shopping trip and the movie, we were heading home. She was clearly exhausted and worn out from the long day of shopping, and probably from life in general. As we were driving through town, she lost focus of the road for just a second and ended up crashing the car. She hit a minivan. On Christmas Eve. Carrying a Jewish family.

The irony didn't escape me, even at that age. My mom wasn't exactly subtle in her feelings about Jewish people. She had her prejudices. My mom was actually racist against everyone. Blacks, Puerto Ricans, Asians. But she especially didn't like the Jews.

I once asked her why she hated the Jews, and she said, "They control the banks."

At that time, we were on welfare, and our cable had been cut off. I remember thinking that we could really use some Jews on our side.

The car was totaled. Just like that, it was gone. It was the only vehicle we had, and we didn't have money sitting around to replace it. We came home from that accident feeling crushed. Not physically hurt, but emotionally beat down. Christmas morning came, and instead of joy or celebration, we were facing the reality of having no transportation, no backup plan, and no real idea of what to do next.

My mom wasn't the kind of person who had safety nets. She was a single mother doing the best she could. Improvising as life threw curveballs her way. She was already drowning. Reaching up for a hand that wasn't there to save her.

One thing my mom *did* love, though, was playing the lottery. It was her ritual, her small slice of hope. Every day, she played the New York State Pick Four: 9-5-6-1—her birthday numbers, as she was born September 5, 1961.

She'd play my birthday: 4-1-8-2, and she also played the Pick Three using my sister's birthday: 3-2-6. She was consistent, superstitious even.

And then, in some twisted cosmic joke, the Pick Four hit that very Christmas Day. Straight. 9-5-6-1. The payout was $5,000, just enough to buy a new car. Exactly what we needed. It was as if the universe dangled a lifeline in front of us, and then, just as quick, yanked it away.

My mother hadn't played her numbers that day.

She had been too overwhelmed. Between shopping all day, watching the movie, then getting into the accident, she had simply forgotten to play. I remember the moment my sister ran in from our aunt's house, full of excitement:

"Oh my God, Mom, your numbers came out straight!" she shouted.

The energy in the room shifted in an instant. My mom just crumpled to the floor and started sobbing. Deep, gut-wrenching sobs. She had forgotten to play the numbers, and it broke her. It wasn't just missing the money. It was everything that moment represented: One more cruel twist of fate. One more missed chance. One more blow to someone who already felt like life was stacked against her. It hit her hard. Right in the face. And I just stood there, watching, helpless.

My mother's lottery ritual gave my sister another opportunity to play a prank on her. This one was particularly cruel which probably made it that much more hilarious. This was a day where my mother did remember to play the lottery. This was for a big jackpot. The winner would get millions. They used to pull the numbers live on television every night during a commercial break when *Wheel of Fortune* or *Jeopardy* was on. One night, my mother had to use the bathroom or something and she gave her lotto tickets to my sister and said:

"Write down the winning numbers when they come on for me."

So, while my mom was in the bathroom, my sister got an idea. Instead of writing down the actual winning numbers from the TV, she wrote down the numbers our mom had picked. She copied them directly from one of her tickets.

My mother came back to check the numbers, and was matching each one to the ticket:

"Sixteen…sixteen…twenty-four…twenty-four…thirty…thirty." She was matching each number and growing more and more excited. After matching all six numbers, she thought she had actually become a multi-millionaire. She was elated, and didn't notice my sister rolling around on the floor cackling like a lunatic.

After jumping up and down—and probably fantasizing about the house she was going to buy, the new car, the lavish clothes and trips—and after imagining every problem going away, she noticed my sister. Immediately, my mother broke down crying.

"You piece of shit!" she whispered.

She then solemnly locked herself in her bedroom, reality setting back in, and didn't speak to my sister for weeks. A big part of who my mom was involved talking to people. She would chat up old Jewish ladies at Bruno's. Having conversations and being social was part of the gig. But she just couldn't do that anymore.

When the radiation stopped working, the doctors offered chemo, which she refused. At one point, they wanted to remove her entire voice box and parts of her throat, which would have left her unable to swallow. She would've needed a feeding tube. She didn't want that either.

She wouldn't be able to have her chocolate-covered cheesecakes. I think it was at that point where my mom had given up. You could feel the bitterness settle in. There was no fight left.

## CHAPTER 10

# GROUND AND POUND

At the time of my mother's cancer diagnosis, I was going to Farley Middle School, which was made up of mostly White kids, and located in Stony Point, New York. I was kicked out in sixth grade for getting into three fights in the first half of the year. I don't know if it had anything to do with my mother's diagnosis, but I was starting to show an angrier side to my personality.

When I went to Farley, I stood out as the poor Brown kid among a sea of rich White kids. My mom had used a friend's address in Stony Point to register me for the school. It was considered a better middle school than Haverstraw. She was trying to look out for me, but she was also setting me up for failure.

My first fight there was with a popular kid named Paul Altieri. My mom was in hairdressing school, and I asked her to cut my hair. I had just seen the movie *Kickboxer* and thought Tong Po's hairstyle, shaved head with a long braid, was badass. I put my own spin on it: I wanted a long braid on one side at the front. My hair was already long, so I asked her to shave everything but a patch in front.

Because I had kinky hair, it just turned into a ridiculous poof ball. Not long enough to braid, just sitting there like a mushroom cloud on the side of my forehead. I showed up to school with that haircut, and while I was at my locker, Paul said:

"Holy shit, Luis. Your hair is gay."

He wasn't wrong. It was, in fact, the gayest haircut anyone had ever seen. But I saw red and started swinging. I was able to get in a punch before a teacher broke it up. We were both sent to the office, and I got suspended. Paul didn't get in trouble. The principal probably agreed with him that my hair was gay.

I had my mom shave it off that night.

My second fight was with another popular kid named Brian Schnell. He'd always been cool to me, but one day I was arguing with this big, loud Black chick. I don't even remember her name, just that she was one of the few other Brown kids at Farley. I was always a shit-talker, class clown type, and we just didn't get along.

During lunch, she started going off on me, and I gave it right back. It was two minorities going at it, and the White kids were loving it. Then she got aggressive and actually wanted to fight. She shoved me. I backed up, and then someone pushed me hard from behind and I went flying right into her.

That's how a lot of fights started back then. Someone would escalate it with a push, and once contact was made, it was on. I turned around, and it was Brian. I wasn't about to fight a girl, so all my anger transferred to him, and I started swinging. I didn't land anything solid, and the fight got broken up quickly. Once again, I got suspended. Brian didn't.

My last fight at Farley was totally my fault. I had a size advantage over most of the kids in my class. I was at least six inches taller than most sixth graders, and I started becoming a bit of a bully. It was mostly just verbal, making fun of kids, talking shit. I was insecure and had been bullied before, so I was just paying it forward. That's how bullies are made. Usually it's parents, siblings, or other kids that beat it into you.

One day in the lunchroom, I was talking shit to a kid I didn't like. I spilled his milk onto his tray. Classic bully move. He didn't react, but his best friend did. I don't remember his name. Just a small African immigrant with a thick accent.

The African kid jumped up, double-legged me to the ground, mounted me, and just started pounding my face while the whole school watched and cheered. It was humiliating. I couldn't move. It felt like a car was on my chest. I had never seen that style of fighting. This was before the UFC became popular. No one had ever heard the term "ground and pound" before.

We both got suspended, but that time I got kicked out entirely. One of the secretaries lived next door to the woman whose address my mom used, so they knew I didn't live in Stony Point. My sister got to finish out her last year there, but I was sent to Haverstraw Middle School.

I fit in much better at Haverstraw Middle School. The school was made up of like 90 percent Hispanic kids. All Puerto Rican and Dominican. Like when I moved to Railroad Avenue, I was surrounded by kids that looked like me and were from similar backgrounds. There were White kids at HMS too, but they weren't as stuck up as the Farley kids.

Back in the '90s, racism just didn't seem like as big of a deal. People recognized differences, but it didn't really matter. I remember my gym coach at HMS would split us up racially during games like basketball. He'd put all the White kids on one team, and all the Black and Hispanic kids on the other team. Then he'd say, "It's the United Nations versus The Great White Hopes."

The White kids would get crushed every time. Everyone just thought it was funny. No one got offended, and no parents called to complain.

Just to keep the streak going, I got into a fight on my first day at HMS. There was a kid named Jeff Lopez who was as big as I was. We exchanged words while lining up after recess. I had a chip on my shoulder and thought I was tough. I swung at Jeff, he ducked, and cracked me in the jaw. I saw stars. The lunch monitors ran over, and we both claimed we were just play fighting, so we didn't get in trouble.

That ended my brief career as a bully. I wasn't cut out for it.

CHAPTER 11

# LOVE HURTS

My mother used to give me regular beatings for just about anything. Not spankings, not a slap on the hand or backside. For as long as I can remember, she didn't just hit me, she beat me like I owed her money. She would box me with closed fists. I remember being a kid and thinking, *What the fuck is wrong with you? I'm a child. You can't just beat up children.* That thought has always stuck with me.

I once knocked over a cup of milk when I was seven. My mom clenched her fist and punched me straight in the face. No warning. No time out. Just a closed-fist punch from a grown woman to a little kid. If I talked back, she wouldn't hesitate to grab a belt and whip me until she got tired.

To this day, I practice peaceful parenting with my son. He's never been spanked or even threatened with any kind of violence. We are adults. They are kids. It's our job to protect them.

Violence was a regular part of my childhood for as long as I can remember. When I was little, I was helpless. But as I got older, I realized I could defend myself.

I was around twelve, maybe in seventh grade, and I had stayed out late, till like 1:00 a.m., talking to a girl from the neighborhood. This was back before everyone had a cell phone. I had a beeper, which was kind of a status symbol back then.

Kids walked around with them clipped to their belts like they were doctors or drug dealers. It was more of a fashion trend than a functional tool to communicate with each other. Someone would page you, then you'd have to find a payphone to call them back. It was very inconvenient.

My mom had been beeping me over and over for a couple hours, and I was just lost in this conversation with this skank from my neighborhood. Her name was Crystal.

(Side note: I've never met a girl named Crystal that wasn't trouble. Crystal ended up being my girlfriend that year, and at a party she refused to kiss me during a game of Truth or Dare. She kissed other guys, just not me. That relationship was doomed from the beginning.)

I finally looked at my beeper and saw a dozen pages from my home number, and said to myself, out loud, "FUCK!"

I got home, and she was already a mess: pacing, crying, panicked. She thought I was dead. She had convinced herself I'd been abducted or killed or lying in a ditch somewhere.

Seeing me alive sent her into a full-blown rage. I was home and safe. Her reaction wasn't relief. It was violence!

She came at me with tears streaming down her face, screaming, shaking, and swinging. What did she do with the news I was alive? She tried to beat the shit out of me.

That was my mother's logic: If she was scared, she hit. If she loved you, she hit. If you failed a test, if you talked back, if you stayed out late, if you made her worry, she hit. She wanted me to do well in school, to be successful, to stay safe. And in her mind, the best way to teach me any of that was through beatings.

It was a complicated dynamic. She loved me deeply, desperately even, but it came out in fucked up ways. She didn't know how to nurture or guide or explain; all she knew was survival. She had endured worse than what she was putting us through, so in her own twisted, abusive logic, she believed she was giving us a better life than the one her parents gave her.

By this point, I wasn't that little kid anymore. I was getting bigger, stronger, and I was done just taking it. I didn't swing back, but I stood my ground. I pushed her off me and I yelled back.

They say if you encounter a black bear in the woods, you should make yourself bigger and try to scare it off: "If it's black, fight back."

That's how I started to see it. When I was younger, I treated her more like a brown bear: "If it's brown, lay down." But now I wasn't laying down anymore.

I want to be very clear: I would never, ever hit my mother. But after years of enduring beatings, I had figured out how to protect myself. I could block most of her blows or hold her wrists so she couldn't hit me. When you're little there is only so much you can do to protect yourself but now I was bigger and stronger than her and my own survival instincts were kicking in.

Her go-to weapon was always a belt. She'd use wire hangers, curtain rods, wooden spoons, and really anything she could get her hands on, but the belt was her favorite. My sister used to treat the whole thing like some kind of sick sport. She'd watch like she was watching gladiators in the Colosseum.

She'd root for my mother excitedly and laugh when the belt would crack. She'd even help my mother with the belt selection. My mother would be getting worked up, and my sister would run to her bedroom and grab the most painful belt she could find.

This wasn't just one old leather belt from a closet. My mom had an arsenal. Studded belts, plastic belts, belts with metal spikes, belts you wouldn't even wear unless you were going to a punk concert. I don't know where she got them all, but she had so many belts. She didn't even wear them. I think she had them exclusively to beat my ass.

When she would start getting worked up, my instinct was always the same: dive under a blanket, build a makeshift fort with my knees and elbows, a kind of soft armor. It didn't stop the blows completely, but it dulled them, spread them out. Eventually, she'd get tired. She had no stamina.

She was a recovering drug addict who never worked out and survived on cheesecake.

Sometimes I'd wedge a wooden bat between the door and the radiator in my room to create a makeshift barricade, just enough to keep her out until she got tired and moved on.

That night where I stayed out till 1:00 a.m. was the first time I saw her not just as my mom, but as something more complicated, someone deeply unstable, unpredictable, and hurting in ways which were hard to understand. She loved me so much that the thought of losing me drove her to hurt me. That is fucked up. For all the bullshit, there was still love there. A confused, distorted kind of love, but love all the same.

As I said before, Mike lived on the corner of Route 9W and Railroad Avenue. It was a sharp, busy intersection. Route 9W cuts through a huge swath of New York—a serious road with trucks and speeding cars.

One winter afternoon I was hanging out with Mike. This particular day, it was freezing cold. But back then, nobody cared if it was twenty degrees. Kids just went outside. Parents generally didn't give a shit.

Mike and I were playing a dumb game where we tried to outrun the spinning electric meter on the side of his house. One of us would watch the dial, and the other would race around the house, trying to make it back before the wheel completed a turn. It was ridiculous, but it made us giggle like little assholes. We were both really competitive. We treated it like it was the Olympic trials.

I took my turn and tore around the corner too fast. I slipped on the icy walkway and smashed my face, specifically the bridge of my nose, against the sharp edge of the front steps. It split right open. Blood gushed down my face like a faucet had been turned on. Mike panicked and bolted. Didn't say a word, just took off running to get help.

He brought back his mom, who called 911, and the ambulance came quick. The cops didn't explain much when they called my mom. Just told her, "Your son's been injured and is being taken to the hospital." No details, no reassurance. Just that. And my mom, hearing that, assumed the worst: that I'd been hit by a car on Route 9W. That stretch of road terrified her. She grabbed my sister, telling her that I had been hit by a car. They both dug my mom's shitty car out of the snow. There had been a snow storm the day before and my mother's car was buried. It took them over an hour.

By the time they made it to the hospital, I wasn't there. I was back at Mike's house. The ambulance was waiting for my mom before they took me to the ER. They had miscommunicated or something. My mom just heard the word hospital and lost it.

When my mom showed up at Mike's, her and my sister were a mess. Covered head to toe in mud and soaking wet. They had tears frozen to their cheeks. I was sitting on the couch with a bandage on my nose, drinking hot chocolate like nothing happened.

I ended up going to the hospital and needing thirty stitches on my nose.

Looking back, I know she wanted to keep me from going too far down the wrong path. In her own twisted, broken way, she thought she was saving me. Even if it was a bat-shit crazy way of doing it. Regardless, the beatings never stopped.

My mother and sister would also get into brutal fights. The difference between my sister and me was that she would actually fight back. I was taught never to lay my hands on a woman by the same woman who was regularly beating the shit out of me.

My sister also got nosebleeds very easily. If you tapped her nose, it would start bleeding like crazy. If she was thinking too hard, it would bleed. I remember one time my mother and sister got into a full-on drag-out fight. Who knows what it was even about, but they were really going at it. My mother, weaponless, was doing her best Mike Tyson impression, bobbing side to side and throwing power shots. My sister tried to keep up, but she was only twelve. At one point, my mother cracked her hard, right in the nose, and just like clockwork it started gushing blood.

But because my sister has always been a savage, she didn't cry. What she did next took such massive balls that I still can't believe she did it. The fight happened in the living room. My mother had just financed a new living room set with my aunt's co-signature. It wasn't particularly nice.

Probably the cheapest set you could get at Seaman's. But it was new, and it was ours. My mother rarely had money for nice things. The one time she got a new car, it was a Dodge Neon. Probably the shittiest car you could buy new at the time. It was zero down and ninety-nine dollars a month, and somehow, she still got behind on payments.

So, after getting punched, my sister looked my mother dead in the eyes and started wiping the blood from her nose and mouth with her hands. Then she wiped it all over the brand-new couch. My mother's jaw dropped. She couldn't believe it. My jaw dropped. I couldn't believe it. While my mother was frozen in shock, my sister ran to her bedroom, locked the door, and didn't come out for two days.

Another time, when I was in the ninth grade, my mother was beating me again, likely because I refused to do my homework. I didn't do a single homework assignment for my entire high school career, and it drove her nuts. My ADHD wouldn't (and still doesn't) let me do work I don't enjoy. If I like the work, I dive in headfirst and never come up for air. If I don't, I just don't do it.

My mother was starting to get worked up, and I was sitting on that same blood-stained couch, rolling my eyes at her. My sister was sitting next to me, watching the spectacle like it was a sporting event. If she'd had a big foam finger that said "#1 Mom," it would've matched her energy perfectly.

As my mother got more heated, she grabbed a broom from the kitchen. In true Denise M. Painter fashion, it was the cheapest broom possible, a thin metal hollow tube with a broom head screwed on. She started hitting me with the stick end, and it snapped in half against my arm. Now, one end was just a thin metal tube with a sharp point.

Even more pissed that she broke her broom, she started using the broken piece to hit me. Honestly, it was better sized for beatings, shorter than a bat, and easy to get a grip on.

Eventually, I grabbed the broom and yanked it away from her. It was pure instinct. But as I pulled it from her, the sharp end stabbed my sister in the cheek, peeling back a big chunk of her skin. She grabbed her face and screamed. Blood poured down her cheek and onto that poor couch, all over again.

Immediately, I started bawling. I wouldn't cry when my mother hit me at that age, but seeing my sister injured like that broke me. I felt this intense wave of guilt crash over me. I felt like it was my fault. And honestly, as I write this, I still carry some of that guilt. My mother shouldn't have been violent, but maybe I could've tried harder in school. I don't know. I just wanted my sister to be okay.

As I mentioned before, she was already painfully shy. She didn't have many friends, and wasn't planning to go to prom or date anyone. She was quiet and insecure. And now, she was going to have this nasty scar on her face, and it was my fault.

We went to the emergency room, and my mother made up a story about her falling on the steps. When we got home, my sister had about forty stitches in her cheek. For the rest of high school, she wore her hair over her face to hide the scar.

## CHAPTER 12

# TURTLE POWER

For as much time as my sister and I spent fighting with my mother, there were times where she genuinely did try. Even though she had her limitations, she did have moments where she came through.

There was one Christmas in particular that comes to mind. It was the year I asked for a turtle. I can't even say exactly why I wanted one so badly. Maybe it was the fantasy of having something alive that was mine, something I could take care of, something I could name. Or maybe it was just a byproduct of being completely obsessed with the *Teenage Mutant Ninja Turtles*, like every other kid in the early '90s. Michelangelo was my favorite, the goofball party dude who still kicked ass. Every kid my age loved Michaelangelo.

So, that was all I talked about leading up to Christmas: I want a turtle. Just one turtle. Christmas morning came with its usual chaos, torn wrapping paper flying through the air, boxes ripped open with little regard for saving the paper, bows crumpled and forgotten on the carpet. I tore through gift after gift: socks, off-brand action figures, clothes that I knew I'd never wear. Maybe a pair of pajamas in a pattern I didn't like. The usual stuff. But no turtle.

With each opened gift, I felt my chest sink a little lower. It was that kind of gut-punch disappointment only kids really feel on Christmas: The one day of the year when you think, maybe today, just this once, I'll get exactly what I wanted. And then you don't. And it hits hard. But then, like something out of a made-for-TV movie, my mom suddenly said:

"Hey, wait a minute. Isn't there one more box behind the tree?"

My heart jumped. It was like someone had hit reset on my hope. I scrambled to the back of the tree and found it: A small, beat-up cardboard box with a couple of holes punched into the top. I knew what it was before I even touched it. That's the kind of box they give you at the pet store when you buy something that breathes.

I opened it slowly, cautiously, like I was uncovering treasure. And there he was. A real, live turtle. I couldn't believe it. My mom actually came through. I named him Michelangelo on the spot, and in that moment, I was the happiest I had been in a long time. I felt proud, responsible, and grown up. This was my pet. My little green companion. I envisioned the adventures we'd have. Unfortunately, at that time, there was no way of knowing just how short those adventures would be.

Because as it turned out, my mom had bought only the turtle. No food. No tank. No lamp. No little plastic rock for him to sit on. Not even a shallow dish for water. Just the turtle and the box he came in. It was like someone gave me a car with no gas, no keys, and no idea how to drive. I didn't know any better, I was just a kid. I figured, "Okay, I'll make this work."

So, I went outside, pulled up a bunch of grass from the yard, and lined the bottom of the box with it. I thought maybe it would make him feel more at home, more natural. But the truth is, he went from a tiny aquarium at the pet store to solitary confinement in a cardboard cell on the floor of a messy kid's bedroom. There was no lamp, no warmth. Just scraps of grass and a few holes for air.

I thought Michelangelo looked lonely. I started thinking about how he probably missed being around other turtles. Maybe he was sad. I didn't know anything about turtles, I just knew what I saw in cartoons. So, I did what I thought was the kindest thing I could do: I decided to get him a friend.

There was this pond not too far from our place, a spot I used to mess around at during the summer, catching frogs and skipping rocks, called Peck's Pond. I went over there, and after a while of searching the edge of the water, I actually found one: A wild turtle. He was about the same size. Maybe a little meaner looking. I scooped him up, proud of myself, and brought him home.

I named him Leonardo. Of course I did. It felt right. Two brothers, reunited under the *Mutant Ninja* family. But I didn't know wild turtles don't necessarily want roommates. I dropped Leonardo into the box with Michelangelo, expecting at the very least a mutual understanding of *you're both fucking turtles,* but what I got instead was straight-up war.

Leonardo went for Michelangelo's head almost immediately, no hesitation. It was vicious. He bit down like he was trying to take his skull off. I stood there, stunned, watching what I'd hope would be a sweet introduction turn into a fight to the death in a goddamn shoe box. I pulled them apart, but the damage was done. Neither turtle looked the same after that.

Now I had two miserable turtles, injured and stuck in a cardboard prison, without a single thing either of them needed to survive. At the time, and mentioned a few chapters ago, I had undiagnosed ADHD. That meant I had no routine, no follow-through, no executive function to speak of. For a few days, I tried my best. I fed them banana peels, apple cores, and lettuce. Whatever I could find in the fridge that seemed "turtle appropriate." (Side Note: Real turtles won't eat pizza.)

But then life distracted me.

School, friends, video games, and fights with my mom. A week went by. Then another. I stopped checking. Stopped feeding. I just…forgot.

One day, out of nowhere, I remembered: Shit! The turtles! I ran to the box and opened it. What I found was something that still haunts me: Both turtles were dead. Stiff. Shriveled. Eyes rotted out. They looked like they had been frozen in time, staring up at the ceiling, maybe toward the heavens. It was like they had died slowly and painfully, locked in the dark, waiting for someone who never came…me.

I stood there, frozen, the guilt hitting me all at once. I had killed them. Not with intent, but through neglect. Through a childish kind of ignorance and a world that didn't give me the tools to succeed.

Looking back now, I think maybe my mom had tried to teach me a lesson. Maybe she thought:

"This will teach him responsibility."

Or maybe she just didn't think it through at all. Maybe she saw the turtle at the pet store, realized it was cheap, and thought it would shut me up on Christmas morning. Either way, she set me up for failure. No instructions. No gear. No help. Just a living creature in a box, handed over to a child, and left to figure it out.

So, no, I don't carry all the blame for the negligent homicides of those two poor testudines (that's what Wikipedia says is the name of their species), but I carry enough. I still think about those turtles sometimes. Michelangelo and Leonardo. Two tiny creatures who didn't ask to be part of my childhood, and definitely didn't deserve to suffer in it.

Rest in peace, little dudes. You deserved better. Live and learn, I guess.

# CHAPTER 13
# GRANDMA CANDY

It wasn't until I was thirteen or fourteen years old that I discovered my mother was a drug addict. She never talked to me about it, ever. Apparently, my sister had known her entire childhood. She told me once that she saw our mother passed out in a car with a needle sticking out of her arm. But she didn't bring any of this up to me until much later in life.

I feel bad that my sister had to carry that burden. She's two years older than me and was always way more aware of what was going on. While I barely remember our father or his death, she remembers him vividly. She says he was very mean to her, and she thinks it was because she had pale skin. The grass is always greener, I guess.

When I was maybe nine or ten, my mother once told me she had smoked weed before. I freaked out, and started crying. I grew up in the late '80s and early '90s when they were shoving D.A.R.E. classes down kids' throats. "Drugs were bad." "Weed was a gateway drug." One puff and you were practically on death row. I didn't want to picture my mother like that. I think she was testing the waters to see how I'd react if she ever told me the truth. After that reaction, she must've decided I couldn't handle it.

She didn't drink. She smoked cigarettes. That was her only vice, or so I thought. Every night, she'd go to bed around 9:00 p.m. after taking her "back medication." It came in a little orange prescription bottle. I never thought anything of it. I just remember thinking it looked like it tasted good, like a melted orange creamsicle.

She'd take it, light a cigarette, and pass out in front of the TV watching *Nick at Nite*. We loved *Nick at Nite*. I grew up on reruns of *The Patty Duke Show*, *The Mary Tyler Moore Show*, *The Dick Van Dyke Show*, and *Green Acres*. One summer night, between eighth and ninth grade, my sister, my mom, and I were watching TV. Maybe *The Simpsons*, *Martin*, or *The X-Files*. During a commercial break, a news promo came on: "Tonight at 10…a new drug looking to replace methadone, as heroin addiction reaches an all-time high in the US…" Then they cut to a conveyor belt filled with little orange bottles.

The same bottles my mom took every night. I looked at her, "You're a heroin addict." She was stunned. Didn't know what to say. "Of course you are," I said. Then I got up and went to my room and cried.

I don't even know why it hit me so hard. It was just… embarrassing. We were already poor and fatherless; I didn't want another scarlet letter stamped on my chest. I didn't want to be the kid with the junkie mom.

After that, it became my go-to weapon whenever we fought. I'd call her a "junkie" or an "addict." I'd throw it in her face just to hurt her. Looking back, I know it embarrassed her deeply. That's why she hid it from me. But the truth is, my mother stayed on her version of "clean" throughout most of my childhood. She took her methadone every night and passed out to *Nick at Nite*. That was the routine. When I was in eleventh grade, her mother, my Grandma Jane, died suddenly. We never got a coroner's report, so I don't know the official cause of death, but she was addicted to pills.

It was probably an overdose. Grandma Jane looked just like my mom, only shorter and a little chubbier. She was my Great-Aunt Anna Marie's sister, and every Thanksgiving and Christmas, like clockwork, she and my mom would get into some vicious screaming match. One would say something mildly offensive, the other would volley it back, and then it'd explode into an episode of Real Housewives of Paterson or something.

My mom resented her mother. She told us all the time, usually while hitting us: "You think this is bad? This isn't half of what I had to deal with!" She once told me, when I was very young, that her stepfather raped her with an axe pressed to the back of her neck. She was a pre-teen. You know…fun family stories.

Even though they fought like animals, my mom really loved her. When Grandma Jane died, it destroyed her. She was already dealing with cancer and no steady income, and this sent her into a deeper depression. Her mother's death was sudden. I guess she still had some things she needed to say. We went to Paterson, New Jersey, to clear out her apartment. It was small and smelled like every old lady's apartment:

medicine and makeup. She didn't have much money, but she was old and weird enough to have some cool shit.

A massive coin collection, tons of Elvis memorabilia, and knickknacks only old people collect. I had just turned sixteen and gotten my license. Lucky for me, she also had a 1990 Buick, and no one to drive it. My Grandma Jane loved me, and I just know she would have wanted me to have that Buick.

While going through her bedroom, we opened a dresser and found drawers full of prescription pills, neatly organized in alphabetical order. Every painkiller and muscle relaxer you could imagine. We later found out at her funeral that she'd been selling them around Paterson.

We affectionately started calling her "Grandma Candy" after that. We didn't realize it at the time, but that day marked the beginning of the end for my mother. She took every single bottle home with her. Trash bags full of pills. That stash lasted her a couple of years, and eventually led her back to heroin.

We figured she ran out of pills, and heroin was just easier to find. She also took Grandma Jane's ID and a few credit cards. Since she looked just like her, she could use them without question. She bought us a camcorder and some furniture, maxed out the cards, and never once considered paying a dime back.

That was my mom.

# CHAPTER 14
# CALIFORNIA LOVE

I've had an interesting relationship with alcohol, well, substance abuse in general. The very first time I tasted alcohol was during my communion. I was about six years old and got a champagne toast. Later, when I was around ten, my sister kept sneaking glasses of wine at Christmas. Probably had two or three. Definitely enough to get a little bit of a buzz going. She thought it was hilarious.

I also remember another time when my Great-Grandma Rose had some beer in the house. It was some gross German beer. I stole one of the cans out of the fridge and me and JR Robinson took it up the block and on the side of a random house on Benson Street. We cracked it open, took a few sips, and it was awful. I ended up leaving it on a street corner and running away from it. Later that night, I actually ratted myself out because I was afraid I'd get caught. I figured it'd be better to confess before the shit hit the fan.

But overall, my early experiences with alcohol were pretty mild. Nothing crazy, just some random, awkward kid moments. One time, I attended a Gomez family function at my uncle's house.

My Uncle Julio, my father's brother, was this big, burly guy. Him and his wife Joyce already had something like ten kids. Eventually, they ended up with twelve or thirteen. Most of them live in New Jersey, and I'm still close with a few of them today. Especially my cousins April and Lisa, who would regularly visit us when we were kids. We were all around the same age.

It's a hilarious family. Every time there's a gathering, it's like an entire tribe of Gomez's. We're all cut from the same cloth—same walk, same talk, raspy voices, hunched shoulders. It's obvious we all come from the same gene pool, and it's kind of surreal to see it all in one place.

So, at this particular family function, I remember my Uncle Julio, sitting on his front porch, drinking something called Anisette, which is a kind of licorice-flavored alcohol. It's truly disgusting. Just a shitty tasting alcohol.

In his gravelly voice, he asked me, "You want a sip?"

I said, "Sure."

As soon as the drink touched my lips, he shouted to my mom:

"Denise, your son's drinking Anisette!" Totally ratted me out.

But stuff like that wasn't really frowned upon in my family. Sometimes if my mother was busy washing the dishes or doing something with her hands, she would ask me to light cigarettes for her. It was almost like substance use, in one form or another, was just part of the culture. It was almost something expected.

Most of my uncles were into drugs. My mom, too. So, it wasn't seen as anything unusual.

Nobody really batted an eye. I didn't get in trouble for stealing that terrible German beer from my grandma. My mom was the one who gave me champagne at my communion. And when Uncle Julio ratted me out for drinking Anisette, everyone just laughed. No one gave a shit. There was this unspoken assumption that my sister and I would probably end up having substance issues, just like everyone else in the family.

I remember the first time I got really drunk, it was New Year's Eve, and I was twelve. I had just moved to Railroad Avenue and my next-door neighbor and friend, Cano, was having a party. Cano was a pretty tough Puerto Rican kid who had a little brother named Miguel, who was also scrappy. This wasn't a kids' party. This was a full-blown adult party that just allowed kids to be there. And we were drinking. Openly. No one cared. Cano's mom and stepdad were right there in the room.

Looking back now, as a parent, it's hard to even process. I was the same age as my son is now. It blows my mind that as I'm writing this my son is downstairs watching a *Spider Man* movie, and eating a sandwich. I can't even fathom him being in a social setting like that. If I walked into that kind of situation today, I'd call the cops. No hesitation. I'd want everyone held accountable for what I now see as straight-up child abuse. But, again, back then, in that environment, it didn't feel wrong. It didn't feel like abuse. It just felt...normal.

Cano's mom had him when she was a teenager. So, by the time we were twelve, she was probably in her mid-to-late twenties. Still basically a kid herself. Everyone there was young, on welfare, and struggling. That was life. You'd go to a party and there'd be adults drinking, kids drinking, and everyone just coexisting like it was no big deal. And in that world, it wasn't.

At that party, I was drinking everything I could get my hands on: wine coolers, beer, regular wine, and hard liquor. I mean, you name it. I wasn't thinking about what mixed with what, or how much I should be drinking. At twelve years old, you don't know how to pace yourself, you don't understand limits, you're just grabbing whatever's in front of you and throwing it back like it's nothing.

I ended up getting absolutely wrecked. Like blackout drunk. As bad as it gets. I was way past the point of a little buzz; I was a stumbling, slurring mess. Just completely out of control.

There were a bunch of older teenagers at the party as well. A handful of kids that were eighteen or nineteen years old. Some of them were affiliated with the Latin Kings, or at least claimed to be. There were definitely some guys there who had been involved with some shit. That kind of low-level gang presence was normal on Railroad Avenue. It was part of what we were all growing up around.

I wouldn't say they were hardcore gangsters. These were mostly wannabe thugs. But still, they were much tougher than us. We were twelve.

One of the guys was this dude with long dreadlocks. He was maybe eighteen or nineteen, definitely older than us, and he had that look like he'd seen and done some real shit. His mom was there too, partying right alongside him.

Looking back now, she probably wasn't even that old, maybe mid-thirties at most. But when you're twelve, anyone over thirty feels ancient. It was wild seeing multiple generations of mostly Latino families all crammed into this little space, drinking, laughing, and partying like none of it was out of the ordinary. Because it wasn't.

As the hours passed and after I had way too much to drink, the older kids started messing with me. Not in a brutal or cruel way, but in that playful, drunk-older-brother-bullying-a-younger-brother way. I was an easy target: a chubby, hammered twelve-year-old, stumbling around, completely out of my depth.

They were teasing me and pushing me around a little while laughing. Someone found a pair of handcuffs (why they were even there, who knows) and they thought it would be hilarious to handcuff me to a metal pole in the middle of the party. I wasn't even mad about it. I was drunk and laughing along with them, not really understanding how fast things could turn south.

At some point, while I was still cuffed to the pole, I looked at the older kid with the dreads, and half-joking, half-trying to act tough, I said, "I'll remember your face, bro." I was slurring, probably giggling.

I definitely didn't mean it as a threat. It was more like the drunk ramblings of a kid trying to be funny. But this dude didn't take it that way. He got real serious, real fast. He looked at me and said, "What?" And before I could even process what was happening, he hit me. I remember feeling myself spin from the force of the hit. I stumbled around, still handcuffed, completely confused. My buddy Mike was there, and I asked him:

"Yo, did he just punch me or slap me?"

And Mike, wide-eyed, said, "Yo, he knocked you, kid."

Before I could even turn fully to react, this guy starts wailing on me. Punch after punch. And that's where my memory cuts out. I don't remember much after the first few blows. No real vivid images, just a blur of movement and noise.

When I finally started to wake up, I noticed the cops were there. They must have been called by someone in the neighborhood or maybe even one of the adults at the party, realizing things had gotten out of hand. I remember while I was talking to the cops, the dread head guy's mom walked up to me and started yelling at me in Spanish. She then slapped me in the face. Right in front of the cops! Jesus Christ lady! I've had enough. You guys win. They ended up bringing me home to my mother. I was bruised but not bleeding, and considering the beating I took, it could have been a lot worse.

And my mom, well, her reaction was almost non-existent. She wasn't screaming. She wasn't crying. She wasn't even particularly mad. She seemed more annoyed than anything. I was brought home at maybe two o'clock in the morning, so she was passed out. In my household, physical punishment was immediate and harsh for small, stupid mistakes. She'd kick my ass for something like spilling a glass of milk, but getting drunk, getting into a fight at a party, and getting taken home by the police? Somehow that wasn't a big deal in her eyes. It was just another night, another small screw-up that didn't even register as a real problem. That was the kind of environment I grew up in. That was the normal.

I remember going to bed that night after the New Year's Eve party still in a drunken haze, my body heavy and disoriented. Somehow, even in the blackout state I was in, I knew enough to lie on my stomach, in the "right" position to avoid choking if I got sick in my sleep. I remembered hearing that Jimi Hendrix died choking on his own vomit. Yet, in my drunken confusion, I turned over onto my back laying face up. I laid there for about thirty seconds, staring at the dark ceiling, feeling the room spin around me.

A small, slurred voice in the back of my mind said, "This isn't right. Turn over you idiot." I turned myself back over onto my stomach just in time, and eventually passed out. When I woke up the next morning, my head was pounding so violently it felt like my skull might crack open.

I stumbled into the living room, still dizzy, where my sister was casually watching MTV. I flopped down next to her, my body aching and my stomach still turning. On the TV, I caught the world premiere of "California Love" by Tupac Shakur. That moment seared itself into my memory. That bright, chaotic beat blasting through my already fragile head.

For years after, even well into adulthood, every time I heard that song, I would get physically ill. A gut-level, nauseous, almost sickened response would wash over me, taking me right back to that brutal hangover. It wasn't just a memory, it was a physical, chemical recoil.

That experience really turned me off to drinking for most of my teen years. I drank a handful of times throughout high school and didn't really start drinking regularly until I was of legal age. I realized early on that alcohol wasn't really for me. It didn't sit right with my body or mind.

## CHAPTER 15

# SALTY BLACKFLOUR

By the time I got to high school, I was getting really into heavy metal. I had always liked metal music, but I had gotten more into hip-hop in middle school. My first concert was actually a Poison concert when I was seven years old. Since my sister was a couple years older than me, she had a lot of influence on the music and television I enjoyed. She loved hair bands like Poison, Skid Row, and Mötley Crüe, and that meant I did too. Also, I had played drums in the school band in eighth grade, which really just meant alternating between a snare and a bass drum with another kid doing the same thing. But it gave me the idea: I wanted to be a drummer in a real band.

While at Haverstraw Middle School I had gotten close with a White kid named John Hickey. I knew John since maybe the first grade and had always been friendly with him, but we started hanging out more regularly in middle school. He was a tall, gangly kid with braces and moppy hair. In the seventh grade, John started taking guitar lessons. He had a cheap amp and just enough gear to get started. John was friends with a chubby ginger kid named Dave Green, who I knew casually from elementary and middle school. Dave was actually super talented. He could play guitar, piano, drums, and saxophone. Everything. He was just good at music in a way most people aren't.

I didn't even have a drum set yet, but we decided we were starting a band.

That summer before ninth grade, I saved up some money and convinced my aunt to give me a couple hundred bucks. I went to this place called the Long Island Drum Center, ironically, not on Long Island. It was in Nyack, New York—and I bought a used four-piece Fibes kit with copper shell covers. It was actually a pretty cool set. I grabbed the cheapest cymbals and hardware I could find.

And just like that, Salty Blackflour was born.

We practiced all summer, mainly covering Nirvana songs—poorly. But we were obsessed. When ninth grade started, we looked for a bassist. That's when we found Dan Preusch. Dan was reasonably talented and—most importantly—he had a space we could practice. I kept my drums in my attic and Dave and John would come over to rehearse, but my mom would get pissed and make us stop after about thirty minutes.

Salty Blackflour stuck together throughout all of high school. We actually ended up getting…well, not good, but decent. Okay, we kind of sucked. But we could play well enough to hold a crowd's attention. Kids in the suburbs were bored, and we gave them something to do. That gave us a bit of a following.

I also started producing shows and doing all the booking for the band. At first, just for Salty Blackflour, but eventually I was booking bigger bands too. We had Coheed and Cambria open for us, back when they were still called Shabutie. Their label made them change the name because, honestly, Shabutie sounded stupid.

We did shows with Sworn Enemy and E-Town Concrete, legit hardcore bands. One time, I booked a show co-headlined by Coheed and Cambria and a band called Bulldoze at a bar called Shotz in Sloatsburg, NY. Bulldoze was made up of big, tough bikers who brought their own crew with them. Coheed and Cambria was this emo, progressive punk band—great music, but not exactly what you'd play to get a room full of bikers hyped.

After Bulldoze's set, Coheed and Cambria took the stage. Their music must've pissed the bikers off because an all-out bar brawl broke out. Bulldoze and their guys just started beating the shit out of the members of Coheed and Cambria and a bunch of teenage emo kids. They pulled out blackjacks and other weapons. Cops came. They shut the place down. The bar got busted for underage drinking and never reopened.

I would do anything to get people to come out to our shows. I was always a good promoter. During morning announcements at school, I'd sneak in official-looking flyers with Salty Blackflour's upcoming gigs. Some honor student would read them aloud, unknowingly promoting our band to the entire student body.

After about a year, Dan Preusch left, and our buddy James Meakim joined as bassist. James was a big fan of the band and would always hang out at our shows. He lived in

Orange County, NY, and went to a different high school than us. I'm still close with James Meakim and Dave Green to this day. Kind of like Legion of Skanks, Salty Blackflour had its own community. We had hardcore fans that would come to every show and it was a great way to talk to chicks.

We played shows at least once a month, at a spot in downtown Nyack called The Back Door (a church anyone could rent), local bars that didn't care we were underage, rock clubs, backyards, parks, and anywhere that would let us play.

Being in that band was my whole identity in high school. It gave me a sense of purpose; it also was the foundation of who I would eventually become as both a performer and a producer. Plus, it was a welcome distraction from all the stuff going on at home and in school.

# CHAPTER 16
# AFTER SCHOOL SPECIAL

By the time I got to North Rockland High School, I already knew everyone. I spent half a year at Farley and two and a half years at Haverstraw, and those schools funneled into NRHS. I wasn't popular, but I was known. I was always unforgettable. Even now, you might love me or hate me, but either way, you'll remember me.

At this point, I was starting to tap into a more punk rock/gothy side of myself. I wasn't punk rock or goth. There wasn't actually a label you could put on me. I was starting to hang out with more White kids and playing music. I would dye my hair and wear eyeliner sometimes. This is when JNCO jeans were popular. I would wear these giant jeans that looked like parachutes. I had a chain wallet and was getting into bands like Marilyn Manson, System of a Down, and Nine Inch Nails.

I ended up getting kicked out of North Rockland High School halfway through the ninth grade. I wasn't that bad of a kid, I just hated school. I was always late and I would cut class during all of the lunch periods. If I had lunch during fifth period, I'd skip fourth and sixth to play hacky sack in the courtyard.

We played "attack hack" or just freestyled and did tricks. In attack hack, you had to keep the volley going for three hits, then kick the sack as hard as you could into someone's body or head. It was the aggressive version of a game usually played by stoners and hippies.

I was damn good. I could stall the hacky sack on different parts of my foot. I could do a jester, a difficult trick that looks like you're jumping and clicking your heels together while kicking the hacky sack. I could do rainbows, head stalls, and knee stalls. I could do "around the world" where you circle the hacky sack with your foot while it's in the air. I was good. I could keep it up longer than most. I enjoyed hacky sack way more than history or science.

The final straw that got me kicked out of school was a lie my science teacher, Mr. Greeley, told. He was a fat, sweaty man with yellow pit stains on his white button-down shirts, and had a face that was always red, like he'd just finished yelling. He was a weird dude.

My first two quarters in his class, I got 85s, which made no sense. It was my first-period class, and I was rarely there. I never tested well, never did my homework, and I don't remember paying attention to a single lecture. Still, I wasn't about to question it. I figured he made a mistake—twice.

One morning, I was in class talking to another kid about anything but Earth Science, and Mr. Greeley suddenly erupted: "Get out!" My school had a special room called "Time Out" for disruptive kids. It was basically a storage closet filled with textbooks and three or four desks. I spent a lot of time in that room. The name alone was insulting, like we were toddlers.

That day, there were maybe two minutes left before the bell. I thought, "Good, I'll get a head start to my next class." I left with a smile and didn't say a word.

The next morning, I was called into the principal's office. Mr. LeGrande, the assistant principal, was a prick. Smug. He was having an affair with the French teacher, Mrs. Morello. They were both married. It wasn't a rumor; they eventually left their spouses for each other.

Mr. LeGrande hated me, and he made it obvious. He showed me a signed statement from Mr. Greeley claiming that after I was sent to Time Out, I had threatened his life. According to the document, I said, "You'll live to regret this." Really? Like I'm some gangster in a 1950s movie? It was cheesy and completely untrue.

I was told I would no longer be allowed to attend school during regular hours. I was being moved to PM school. It ran from 2:00 p.m. to 5:00 p.m., starting just before the main student body was dismissed at 2:16. It was one classroom with kids from every grade, nine through twelve. PM school was the last stop before expulsion. These were actually bad kids. Kids who fought, who sold drugs, who did threaten teachers. As much of a fuck-up as I was, I never even cursed at a teacher. Not once.

No one had ever graduated from North Rockland High through the PM program. Mr. LeGrande looked satisfied when he told me that. Earlier that year, he had told me I'd never graduate, and now, he was making it happen. As he said it, tears welled up in my eyes. Not from sadness but from anger. I did not threaten that teacher. This guy was just a fucking scumbag liar. I begged them to find just one witness to back his story. There were thirty kids in the class. Mr. LeGrande didn't care. The decision was final.

I asked to speak to the actual principal, Mr. Hand. I told him everything. He seemed to have some compassion. I don't know if he believed me, but he either believed me or pitied me. He told me that if I got good grades for a year in the PM program, he'd reinstate me. And just like that, I was out.

A couple months later, while I was in PM school, I found out Mr. Greeley had been fired, about two weeks after my "incident." Why? He wasn't assigning accurate grades. He had a locker full of pills and apparently some psychological issues. That's why I'd gotten those 85s. No one told me anything. My mother threatened to sue the school, but that was just talk. She was always threatening lawsuits she never followed through on.

PM school wasn't actually that bad. I knew some of the kids. My neighbor Cano was in the class, along with a few others I'd grown up with. Most came from situations like mine: single mothers, absent dads, poverty, welfare, and abuse. No one to look up to. No one to inspire us.

I ended up thriving in PM school. Each subject had a workbook, and you'd be assigned a few pages per day, and that was it. It was embarrassingly easy. I just took the workbooks home and completed them all in the first week. Once you were done with the work, you could bullshit for the rest of the day.

I ended up getting 100 percent in every class. I made the Principal's List, which is for students with a 95 percent average or higher, like the honor roll, but more prestigious. They hold a special brunch for those kids, and at first, they wouldn't allow me to come. But my mother went to the school, started huffing and puffing, threatening to blow people's houses in, so they just said fuck it and let me come.

After a year, I had maintained a 100 percent average across the board. I was helping other kids with their work. I never got in trouble. I held up my end of the deal. When we approached the school about having me reinstated, they denied me. Mr. Hand had taken a leave of absence, and he had only ever told me, off the record, that he would reinstate me after a year. Nothing was official, and no one was even going to check with him.

For as much shit as I give my mother, I'll say this: Her crazy came in handy sometimes. Once again, she went in, huffed and puffed, threatened to sue, showed her teeth, and gave them no choice but to let me come back.

# CHAPTER 17

# MAN IN ROAD

After getting out of PM school, I was determined to stay on the straight and narrow. I ended up really submerging myself into Salty Blackflour but I also joined the drama society which definitely had a positive impact on me. Those were generally "good" kids and I needed to be around good kids. The band was playing gigs and I was back in school and figuring out who I was.

We had started to get some gigs and were gaining traction in the local music scene. At this point, I had become really close with John. My mother and John's mother were actually friends, too. His mom was a hairdresser, and they had gone to school together. John's dad was a decorated police sergeant and a big, jacked guy. John was terrified of his father. His parents were a little wary about him hanging out with me, and now I understand why. I wouldn't let my own kid hang out with teenage Luis J. Gomez.

There was a short period where they wouldn't let John hang out with me at all. This was after I got drunk on New

Year's Eve. John's dad had heard about it because the police took me home. Then, that following summer, there was another incident. John was getting picked on by a kid in his neighborhood, and he ended up getting into a fight with him in front of the whole block. The other kid got the better of John, and he was humiliated.

So, what does he do? He runs home, grabs his dad's revolver, and chases the kid down the street with it. Completely nuts. Word spread fast, and of course John's dad heard about it. He came home while I was there and was absolutely losing it. I jumped in like, "No guys…John didn't pull out a gun. I was joking around. I said, 'He's going to get his dad's gun!' And everyone just ran." After that, I wasn't allowed to go over to John's house for about a year.

High School in the '90s was different. We didn't have cell phones and social media to distract us. We were bored suburban teenagers. We were constantly looking for something to do. Most of the time we'd hang out in the KFC or Wendy's parking lot, kicking around a hacky sack and making our own fun.

One of the places we used to explore was Letchworth Village, an old insane asylum. It had been shut down in the early '90s for doing all kinds of unethical stuff to patients. My friends and I would break into the boarded-up buildings and rummage through old patient files. It was genuinely creepy, like something straight out of a horror movie.

Then there was Spook Rock Road, a legendary spot in Rockland County. There's a hill with a giant boulder at the top—everyone just assumed that was the "spook rock." Local legend said a young girl had been murdered there, ritualistically sacrificed by Native Americans. If you parked your car at the bottom of the hill and put it in neutral, it would slowly roll backward, uphill toward the rock. The story was that it was the girl's ghost pulling you back to save her. It actually worked. We used to do it all the time.

Of course, the truth was that it was just a magnetic hill, an optical illusion. The way the terrain and horizon lined up tricked your eyes into thinking you were going uphill when you were really rolling downhill. But this was pre-internet, so we all just went with the ghost story.

One night, we decided to play a prank on a friend named Billy. At the time, I was hanging out with John and Dave, trying to get Salty Blackflour off the ground. We also spent a lot of time with Dave's older sisters, Liz and Emily. Liz was a senior when we were freshmen, and Emily had already graduated. I had the biggest crush on Liz Green. She was pretty and smart, and she'd laugh at my jokes.

The plan was to scare the hell out of Billy. We went to Spook Rock Road with the girls and Billy. The plan was for the girls to dare me, John, and Dave to get out of the car and pee on the rock. While we did that, they would speed off. Everyone was in on it except for Billy. We'd brought a bunch of supplies—fake blood, red food dye, tofu, and macaroni salad. We mixed it together in a bag and it looked like guts. Once the car drove off, we'd cover ourselves in the fake blood and guts and lie down in front of the rock like we'd been murdered. When the girls and Billy came back, we'd be "dead," and Billy would freak out.

We pulled it off around 11:00 p.m. We jumped out, they drove off, and we smeared ourselves with the fake gore, laying out like crime scene victims. A few minutes passed. They didn't come back. Cars would drive by, slowing down as they spotted us, then they would speed off. We were cracking up. When the girls finally returned, Billy just laughed and called us gay.

Then we saw a flashlight moving toward us. Someone in a nervous voice asked if we were okay. I told him we were just pranking some friends. He wasn't amused. "We thought someone was hurt," he said. We grabbed our props, piled into the car, and peeled out.

As we drove away, we saw a dozen cop cars flying toward Spook Rock Road. We'd gotten out just in time. We were laughing until John realized he'd left his book bag at the rock—with his wallet and school ID inside. He started freaking out. If his dad found out about this, he was dead. We waited about half an hour for the cops to clear out, then went back. Thankfully, the bag was still there, untouched.

The next day, there was a tiny article in *The Rockland Journal News*. The headline read: "Man in Road." We were so proud. We had made the papers.

# CHAPTER 18
# CEMETERY GATES

I lost my virginity one week after my sixteenth birthday to Kristen. Kristen was best friends with Alyssa, who was John's girlfriend and my friend from drama society. Kristen was sort of a diet goth, a little more goth than me and my core group of friends, but not quite as goth as the group of goth kids that were the "goths" of North Rockland High School.

In the late '90s, there was always a group of goths at every high school. Looking back, it's actually pretty comical. All of these dudes and chicks wearing black eyeliner and lipstick, pretending to be sad for the sake of it. Just optics. The truth is, most of the goth kids at NRHS had nice homes and not much to actually be depressed about.

My friends and I were goth-adjacent. I had long hair for the ninth and tenth grade, and my mother would put multicolored highlights in it. She never got her license to color or cut hair, but she still took all of the curriculum, so she knew how to do it fine. My hair was almost shoulder-length, but because my father was Afro-Latino, it had a nappy kink to it. I could pick it out into an afro, or I'd wet it down and use hair gel and it would fall almost like Jheri curls. Sometimes there would be green or purple highlights. Sometimes I'd leave them blond.

When I started to have a crush on Kristen, I was actually already dating another girl from a different school, Nyack High School, which was more affluent and more artsy than mine. My girlfriend's name was Claire. She was half Filipino and half White. She was in ninth grade, I was in tenth, and I couldn't drive yet, so my friend James, my neighbor from Railroad Avenue, would drop me off at her house after school so I could fool around with her. She was a straight-A student and kind of nerdy, but she had enormous, beautiful tits, a slim waist, and a very pretty face. We were both virgins, but she was the first girl I actually started to experiment with sexually.

I'd go to her house, and we'd sneak up to her bedroom because her elderly grandmother was always home. We would make out a bunch, and Claire would get naked. I would perform oral sex on her, but I wouldn't let her suck my dick.

In my head, I didn't want my girl to have a dick in her mouth. I didn't want to view her as a slut. The thing is, Claire wanted to suck my dick. She asked almost every time, and I'd say no. Instead, I'd let her give me a dry hand job that never actually finished me off. This was our routine every afternoon for a couple of months.

The reality was that I liked Claire, but I mostly liked her because she was cute and letting me get her naked. We didn't actually have anything in common besides being around the same age.

During this time, I was getting very close with Kristen.

Since she was best friends with Alyssa, Kristen would hang out every day after school while we rehearsed for our school musical. The truth is, I only joined drama society because I thought it would be funny. I did that a lot. I liked doing things people didn't expect me to do. I joined the chess club even though I didn't know how to play chess. I never even learned. I just thought it was funny that "Luis J. Gomez was in the chess club."

Being an individual and being unique was always something that mattered to me. In fact, in our high school class superlatives, it was me and my entire friend group who were nominated for "Most Individualistic." The yearbook had all of the categories: Most Likely to Succeed, Most Spirited, Best Dressed, Best Looking, Most Athletic, but they gave one category to the weird ones. "Most Individualistic" was usually given to a goth kid who dressed like all the other goth kids.

In my class, there were three Salty Blackflour band members: myself, John Hickey (who ended up winning), Dan Preusch (who was the first bassist in Salty Blackflour), and a fourth nominee who was actually a popular kid named Michael Cappaluppo, who played sports and hung out with the cool kids. Those cocksuckers nominated him. The jocks couldn't even let us have our weirdo category.

Me, John, and Kristen would also regularly hang out at Alyssa's house. I was developing a real crush on Kristen. She was very pretty, funny, and had a sort of wild energy about her. She was a fan of Type O Negative and Pink Floyd. I liked hanging out with Kristen a lot more than Claire, and because we went to the same school, I'd see her all the time.

I didn't have the ability to just be friends with a pretty girl. I'm not sure any man does. If a girl is pretty and cool, I'll likely fall in love with her, and that may still be true to this day.

One night, Kristen invited me over to her house. This was still while Claire and I were dating. I would sometimes go to Kristen's just to listen to music and eat pizza. Her parents liked me. They were both drunks and would leave her home on the weekends to watch her little sister, and because they were drunks, they didn't have many rules for her.

On this occasion, Kristen was showing me her favorite Fear Factory album. I actually knew Fear Factor already. I saw them open the main stage at Ozzfest '97. At the time, I hadn't heard of them, and their lead singer, Burton C. Bell, came out. He was a fit, long-haired blond guy. He walked up to the microphone and screamed:

"This ain't no fucking Lollapalooza…"

Then the double bass drum kicked in and they played a killer set. As Kristen was showing me their music, I just played dumb. I wanted to make her feel good, like she was teaching me. She then switched to Type O Negative, who I actually hated, but I pretended to like them, so she'd like me more.

During the song "Black No. 1," we were just kind of zoning out. I don't remember exactly how it happened, but my eyes were closed, and when I opened them, Kristen was kissing me—hard. I was in a trance. This was what a real kiss was. It was the first time I really, really liked a girl and she was kissing me. After maybe thirty seconds, we both pulled away and were like:

"What the fuck? Where did that come from?"

Then we kissed again. And again. And again. We spent the whole night just making out. I didn't try anything more, but immediately I knew I had to break things off with Claire. I was already in love with Kristen.

Claire's birthday was the following weekend, and she was having a small gathering in a park in Nyack where she lived. The plan was to go to her birthday party, wait a few days, then break up with her. I didn't want to ruin her birthday.

I'm not sure what it is, but if I have a problem, I can't get it off my mind. Maybe it's the ADHD, but to this day, if there's something on my mind, I obsessively think about it. If a girlfriend says, "I want to talk to you about something later," it will consume me to the point where I can't think about anything else.

I avoided seeing Claire all week. I couldn't get Kristen off my mind, and I wanted to break things off with Claire and ask Kristen to be my girlfriend. The whole week, I couldn't focus on anything else. It was driving me crazy. The week felt like a month. I'd barely talk to Claire on the phone, and I was talking to Kristen more than ever.

When the Saturday of her birthday finally rolled around, I had this overwhelming guilt come over me. How could I go to this party and just pretend to be a good boyfriend? I did some mental gymnastics in my head, and I concluded the only nice way to handle this would be to break up with Claire. On her birthday. Just hours before her party. I called her.

"Hey, Claire."

"Hi, Luis! I'm so excited to see you today and spend my birthday with you!"

She sounded cheerful. Fuck. This was going to be rough.

"Listen, about that…I don't think I can make it today."

"What? Why not?" she asked.

"Well, not only can't I make it…I don't think I can be your boyfriend anymore."

She was stunned. "You're breaking up with me? On my birthday?"

It was like a cliché about every asshole guy in history.

"Yeah, I'm just not feeling it anymore. We live too far. We're too different."

I didn't have the heart to tell her that I liked someone else. And I didn't really have any other excuse. I was grasping at straws. I even pulled out the:

"Look, it's not you, it's me." I was always a hack.

Claire put on her strongest game face and said, "Fine…if that's how you feel." And hung up.

Claire and I would vaguely stay in touch for a few years after. She ended up blocking me on Facebook years later after I defended Daniel Tosh for making a rape joke that got national attention. She ended up studying at Vassar and becoming a big feminist, I'm assuming. I started arguing with her and her friends on a post about Tosh, and she blocked me.

After Claire was out of the way, Kristen and I became boyfriend and girlfriend. For the most part, we were inseparable. We'd hang out at Alyssa's house and fool around in the closet whenever we got the chance. Kristen was a very sexual girl, and she wouldn't accept no for an answer when it came to sucking my dick. We were both hormonal, horny teenagers, and we were both ready to have sex.

She told me she would let me take her virginity for my sixteenth birthday. Happy birthday to me!

We planned it for the weekend following my birthday. She came over to my house on Railroad Avenue. My mother would typically be in bed by 8:00 or 9:00 p.m. She would take her methadone and pass out in her bed with lit cigarettes. Her whole mattress had cigarette burns in it. How she never burned the entire place down is beyond me.

The plan was for Kristen to come over and for us to hang out by Peck's Pond, which was a ten-minute walk from my house. After my mom went to bed, we would finally do it in my bedroom.

We got to my place, and I set the mood. I had a blacklight and a lava lamp, which were pretty typical for teenagers in the late '90s, and at the time I saw it as sexy mood lighting, as if my bedroom was a cheap strip club.

I put the song "Cemetery Gates" by Pantera on repeat. The song started slow and then broke into a heavy guitar riff during the chorus. In my mind, that was the point where I'd really be fucking her good. I had it all planned out in my head, start slow, then as the song got heavy, really give it to her.

It didn't end up being that smooth. We used condoms, which I stole from my mother's purse. These were cheap, thick condoms that she got from the local health clinic she visited for her methadone. They were terrible. I have always, and will always, hate using condoms. Some people say it's like watching TV with a paper bag over your head. It's worse. It's like you're staring at a wall, thinking there might be a TV in the next room, but you're not really sure. You put your ear to the wall. You think you hear something, but it's all mumbles. It might be a TV. Eventually, you give up.

We ended up having sex for probably a couple of hours with neither of us achieving anything close to an orgasm. That song must have played through thirty times. Either way, it was still pretty cool. I was no longer a virgin, and I lost my virginity to the girl I loved. To the girl I would spend the rest of my life with.

Yeah, right.

Kristen and I ended up breaking up six months later. She started dating a real goth and getting heavily into drugs. She ends up showing back up in my life later on, and we'll get into that.

# CHAPTER 19
# JERK CHICKEN

When I was sixteen years old, I ended up getting a job at KFC. I'd go on to other jobs at Taco Bell and at Blockbuster Video too. I worked on a lot of shitty jobs that teenagers at the time would flock to.

But, for whatever reason, KFC was a job that I just enjoyed. Maybe subconsciously it was because my mother loved it so much. I don't know. I worked at KFC for a little over a year and I ended up getting all of my friends jobs there too. Everybody that was in my rock band, Salty Blackflour. My bassist, my guitarist, my singer, my buddy Gene, my buddy Dan Doherty, it was like, seven or eight of us working at this KFC.

Our boss was this kind of goofy guy named Calvin. He was ex-Navy. Very, what you'd call, "jacked." Muscular and tall. But he was also kind of a dim-witted moron. Despite that, he was our boss.

I remember one time I was sweeping up some fallen chicken and French fries off the floor, and the son of the franchise owner was there. His name was Alex. He and his dad owned probably twenty different KFCs around Rockland County and Jersey.

Now, I'm sweeping up, and as I'm doing it, Alex comes up and looks at me with a very serious face and says:

"Why are you sweeping?"

And I was like, "Oh, um, it's dirty."

And he says, "Who told you to sweep?"

I replied, "Nobody."

And at that second, his tone shifted, his face brightened up, he grabbed me by the arm and brought me around to everybody in the shop. And he was like:

"This is the type of work ethic we need. You don't need to be told to do things. You guys gotta be able to do it and go above and beyond."

And he gave me a twenty-five-cent raise. I was making \$5.25 an hour, and it went up to \$5.50 an hour. It was actually a very formative "oh shit" moment for me. I liked getting praised for being a hard worker and I liked making money even more.

My buddy Dave Green and I were an unstoppable force at KFC. We worked the drive-thru like a well-oiled machine. Dave would be the one talking to customers through the headset at the register, while I packed the orders with lightning speed.

We turned it into a game, challenging ourselves to see how fast we could complete each order. A customer would pull up to the drive-thru intercom and rattle off something like:

"I'd like to order a three-piece original with coleslaw, a biscuit, three strips with potato wedges, green beans, a corn muffin, a Diet Coke, and a regular Coke."

While they were still ordering, I was already stuffing food into boxes like a madman. By the time they drove the ten yards to the pay window, their bag of food was ready and hanging out the window like a magic trick. People were astonished. They couldn't believe it was possible.

We made work fun by treating it like a competition. The goal was simple: Get that bucket of food out the window before the customer even got there. And for me, it actually was fun.

At that point in my life, I felt like I was being pulled in two completely different directions. On one hand, I was the poor kid with a drug-addicted mom and a murdered pimp father, headed down the same dangerous road they'd walked. On the other hand, I was learning to be a responsible, self-reliant young adult who took pride in having a strong work ethic and making an honest paycheck.

Even though it was just fast food, I was proud of being the best at something, even if that "something" was packing buckets of chicken faster than anyone else. When we found out our KFC had higher numbers than the one a few towns over, we knew that success was because of our hustle, and that felt good.

But then there was our goofy manager, Calvin. Turns out, he was sleeping with one of the other employees, who may or may not have been of legal age at the time. She had braces and was clearly young. It was a gross situation. Back then you could get working papers and a part-time job at fourteen with your parents' permission, so it wasn't unusual for someone that age to be employed. But still, it was messed up.

Maybe a year after I quit working there I was smoking a blunt in the parking lot behind the KFC. I was almost eighteen at this point and I had picked up a pretty serious weed habit. While smoking I saw Calvin and this younger girl in his car. The windows were fogged up. Later, I confronted him about it, which led to me basically blackmailing him for free KFC for about a year. I told him I wouldn't say anything as long as he hooked me up with free strips and a mac and cheese for life. It was, in my opinion, a fair deal for all parties involved.

Calvin was a dirtball. But to be fair, so was I at the time. There was one occasion when I was working the drive-thru and decided, for some reason, to go to the bathroom and jerk off—during the dinner rush, no less. With the drive-thru completely slammed.

So, yeah, for all the talk about my great work ethic, I was also a human being. And sometimes humans do questionable things—like sneaking off to the bathroom in the middle of a busy shift to handle business.

For whatever reason, I really took my time in there. I wasn't quick about it at all. I was completely in my own world. Meanwhile, out on the floor, everyone was panicking, asking, "Where the fuck is Luis?"

Our KFC had built a reputation, so when I disappeared, it threw everything off. I remember finishing up, cleaning myself off, and finally opening the bathroom door only to find Calvin standing right there. His face was beet red, and he was fuming.

He didn't yell. He didn't even say anything. He just punched me in the face. That's how mad he was. He literally didn't know what else to do with his anger.

Here's the funny part: He didn't even know I'd been jerking off. He just thought I'd been taking an absurdly long shit. But he was so angry that he hit me. I was only sixteen at the time. Looking back, it really says a lot about the times we lived in.

Nowadays, anyone in that situation would sue KFC, the manager, and the franchise owner. But back then? I just wasn't built that way. In my mind, it almost made sense. I remember thinking, "Well, if you get caught jerking off during the dinner rush, you probably shouldn't be shocked if you get punched in the face."

So, I went back to work. I didn't go home, didn't complain, didn't tell anyone. I just kept working until I eventually left the job for good.

## CHAPTER 20

# THERE'S SOMETHING ABOUT MARY JANE

The first time I smoked weed, I was seventeen years old. I had prided myself on being straight edge all throughout high school. It wasn't that I had a moral issue with weed or drinking, I just thought it made me unique. Most kids my age were partying, and aside from drinking a few times, I liked standing out by not drinking or smoking. It was just a way to be an individual.

One day, out of nowhere, I was hanging out with Dave and James from Salty Blackflour and said:

"Guys, we should try weed. Just to see what it's like. Let's try it."

They both immediately agreed: "Sure. Fuck it!"

The problem was none of us had any idea how to get weed. None of our close friends smoked, and we didn't have a "guy." I lived in West Haverstraw, just a town over from Haverstraw, NY. Haverstraw was full of Puerto Ricans and

Dominicans, it had a rough edge, but it wasn't as ghetto as Spring Valley, which was mostly Black. Still, there was a strong Latino hood culture in Haverstraw in the late '90s. Most people listened to hip-hop, and fights were common. A lot of folks from Haverstraw owned homes and worked hard, but there was still this gritty pride to being Hispanic.

Since I had so many connections in Haverstraw, we figured we'd just drive around and ask. We took my mom's black Dodge Neon and pulled up to bodega and awkwardly asked the old guys behind the counter:

"Got any trees?"

And they'd say, "No. Get out of my store."

We asked teenagers, adults, kids I knew and didn't know. Nothing. We spent the entire day trying to score and came up empty. Then I remembered my Uncle Raymond was crashing with my Aunt Anna Marie at that time. He had been in and out of prison his whole life. He was a major pothead. He had to know someone who sold weed. Eventually, Raymond developed paranoid schizophrenia and believed he could talk to God and angels. Maybe he could. Maybe it was the weed.

The next morning, I asked him if he could get us some weed.

"Of course!" he said.

Potheads love getting other people high for some reason. He said he needed twenty dollars and would get us two dime bags of some low-grade weed. He'd roll us two joints from one of them and keep one joint for himself as payment. We held onto the second dime bag.

Around noon, we went to the kiddie playground at West Haverstraw Elementary. That's where teens usually got high.

Some people say that you don't get high your first time smoking. But I shit you not, I have never been higher in my life.

We lit the joint and at first, I just felt lightheaded. Then I took a step, felt my foot hit the ground, and started dying laughing. Walking was suddenly the funniest thing in the world. I tried to explain it to Dave and James, but I was gasping between laughs. We were all just rolling around on the ground like stoned idiots.

That night, we had tickets to SnoCore, a concert tour featuring System of a Down, Incubus, Puya, and Mr. Bungle. My aunt drove us from her house, near the school, to my friend Chicky's place. His parents were driving us to the show in Asbury Park, New Jersey.

What should've been a seven- or eight-minute drive turned into almost an hour, because we were so high we kept giving her the wrong directions. We'd tell her to turn right, when we meant turn left, then we'd break down laughing. I remember pressing my face against the window, tears streaming down from how hard I was laughing. My aunt was yelling:

"What's wrong with you?! What's wrong with you?!"

And we just kept howling. That night was incredible. Nothing like alcohol. My first experiences with drinking were disasters. But weed? That first high was joyful. It was with my best friends, people I trusted and created with. We laughed, we saw our favorite bands, and we experienced music in a brand new way.

If that first time had gone badly, if we'd gotten caught or something terrible happened, maybe I wouldn't have become a pothead. But it went so right that it became part of my life from that moment on.

## CHAPTER 21

# BIG TONY AND BOURBON JACK

From the ages of sixteen to eighteen, my life revolved around two things: my band, Salty Blackflour, and my new girlfriend, Vicky. She was a nice Ukrainian chick from a wealthy family—very normal, fairly attractive, and a genuinely good influence on me. Vicky was a solid student, and she had her sights set on going to prom. The school required at least a C average to attend, and that was basically the only reason I made it through eleventh and twelfth grade. I didn't want to see her go to prom with some other dude.

I did my best to come off like a good guy around her and her family, but the truth was, I was hiding a whole other side of myself. During my senior year, I started smoking weed every day. She had no idea. I kept it from her for two full years. Same with the fact that I was hustling to make money on the side.

The band was going strong, and I was booking gigs, producing, and promoting our own shows, but it wasn't enough to pay the bills. Minimum wage jobs weren't cutting it either. So, I started looking for other ways to make cash.

I was still willing to steal. I was still willing to make money in whatever way I could, and I started doing a lot of petty crimes and petty theft. I was working at a place called Big Tony's Pizza at the time, just a few stores down from the KFC. I worked at so many different spots right in that same area. Funny enough, I had already worked for Big Tony's Pizza once before, back when I was about twelve years old with my friend Mike.

Back then, we were supposed to be delivering flyers and putting them on people's doors. That was the whole job. But by the second day, we had already decided we were over it. Instead of walking door-to-door handing out those flyers, we looked at each other and said, "Fuck this!" We took the entire stack, walked to the Low Land Bridge in Stony Point, and just dumped them all right over the side. Then we went back to the shop like nothing happened and collected our pay.

Of course, the owner found out almost immediately. Someone called the pizzeria to complain that there were thousands of his flyers scattered all over the park below Low Land Bridge. We were instantly fired from that job. But even after that, it was still our local pizzeria, and we'd go in there all the time. We were still on friendly terms with the owner, a shady character named Tony.

I think most pizzeria owners are basically wannabe mobsters. They all want to be "that guy," the connected guy who could fit right into a real-life version of *The Sopranos*. Tony was exactly that type. A few years later, when I was a senior in high school, he hired me back to deliver pizzas.

But delivering pizzas wasn't all Tony had me doing. He would also give me "assignments," which basically meant stealing stuff. He'd ask his friends what size sneakers they wore and then pass those measurements along to me. He'd say things like, "I need a size seven female, a size nine female, a size thirteen male."

I'd then head over to Modell's, which was a big sporting goods store in the tri-state area, and I'd rip the sensors off the sneakers and just walk right out with them. I was already somewhat familiar with how to get away with this and exactly what the staff's response would be if they happened to catch me in the act.

See, right before I was rehired at Big Tony's, I had briefly worked at a clothing store called Hot Topic. It was like Abercrombie for Goth Kids. It was on the third floor of the Palisades Center Mall which was a newer mega-mall in West Nyack, NY. It was huge. Four floors. At the time, it was the third largest mall in the country. It had a fucking Ferris wheel!

On just the second day of training at Hot Topic, they were teaching us what to do if we spotted a shoplifter. They told us:

> *"If you see a shoplifter, just step in front of them but keep your hands at your side. DO NOT TOUCH THE PERPETRATOR. If you touch them and they get hurt, they can sue the store. You have to call security. When security arrives, they also can't put their hands on them. They have to verbally detain them until the cops arrive."*

And in my head, I'm thinking, *Oh, well, that's insane.* Why would anybody wait for the cops?

So, I quit that job at Hot Topic almost immediately and started robbing the mall instead.

Me and my friend Vinny had a whole system. Twice a month, at around two o'clock in the morning, we'd sneak into the Palisades Center Mall. The mall's entrance doors would always be unlocked because the ice-skating rink and movie theater stayed open late.

Once inside, we'd head straight to the Rainforest Café's big wishing well and completely clear it out. Every single cent. We would show up with plastic shopping bags and fill them with the wishes of other kids. It was like that scene in *The Goonies*, only we had no moral compass that told us to stop.

We knew that even if security caught us in the act, the worst they could do was call the cops, and by the time the cops actually showed up, we'd already be gone. Each time we did this, we'd walk away with a couple hundred dollars to split.

We would bring the bags of wet change home and dry the coins out on my bed for a day. You had to do this. The first time we knocked off a wishing well, we actually broke the Coinstar machine at the supermarket by filling it up with wet coins. It started smoking and we had to dip out and waste our score.

So now, I was deep into these petty crimes, but at the same time, I was still doing musical theater, still in my band, and I had a girlfriend, Vicky, who had no idea that any of this was happening. She didn't know I was committing crimes. She didn't know I was starting to smoke weed and becoming a pothead. I kept every bit of it from her.

I was basically living a double life, being pulled in two completely different directions. Again. My father was rubbing off on me.

This was all happening when I was just turning eighteen years old. I had just barely graduated high school. At the time, I remember I was working as a bouncer at a place called Bourbon Jack's, which was an underage drinking spot. This place was literally just filled with fifteen-, sixteen-, and seventeen-year-old kids.

The owner's business model was to open up a place where underage people could drink. The bartenders would get fined, he would pay their lawyer fees and fines, get shut down, and open up again under a different name.

This place was packed seven nights a week. Everybody that I knew from high school was hanging out there. I ended up getting fired from that job because people were getting into fights every night. Kids that I knew and grew up with were getting in each other's faces, and I'd have to try to break it up, which I always wanted to do nonviolently.

One time, the owner saw this and said to me:

"What are you doing?" And he grabbed my flashlight, and he was like, "Break this up! Hit him with the fucking flashlight!"

I was like, "I'm not going to hit a kid over the head with a flashlight, dude. We were in the Cub Scouts together." And that's when he let me go. I was fired.

I was working security at Bourbon Jack's while at the same time I was delivering pizzas for Big Tony's and getting "assignments" from the owner, Tony, to steal sneakers, golf clubs, bowling balls—all this crazy shit.

I would walk in with empty shopping bags. Then I'd fill them up with as much stuff as possible. I was obnoxious about it. I didn't even try to hide it. I would just walk out of the store with bags full of stuff. Security would sometimes see me and say:

"Stop!"

I'd say, "No!" And just keep on walking.

That was that. No one ever stopped me. No one ever grabbed me. No one ever did anything. Then, one day, Tony asked us if we wanted to make some "real money." Both me and my friend James from Railroad Avenue were working there. He proposed that we come in at night when the pizza shop was closed and burn it down so he could collect the insurance money. He would give us $5,000 each! Neither of us had ever seen that much money before so we were like "Let's party!" We were idiots.

The plan was for James to come to Bourbon Jack's on a night I was working, and we'd make sure to be on the security camera for our alibi. James was going to come and drink a little bit, hang out, and then we'd sneak out the back during my shift.

It was about a twenty-minute drive to the pizzeria. When we got there, we were going to take lighter fluid, spray the electrical fuse box with it and then light that baby up. Because in our mind, if we lit the electrical fuse box, the fire would travel through the wires and burn the entire place down. After which, we'd drive back to the bar, get ourselves seen on camera again and we'd have our alibi.

It was the biggest horse-shit plan anyone could ever come up with. We were really ready to do it. We were ready to go. It was the night of the job, and Tony called us up and called off the plan. He didn't want to go through with it. And that was the only reason we didn't do it.

I don't know, maybe you can call it divine intervention, but I thank God Tony called it off. I was fully prepared to make a really, really bad decision that would have likely ruined my life.

## CHAPTER 22

# THE INSIDE JOB

At this time in my life I was starting to make some bad decisions. I was getting more desperate for money and I was getting more ballsy with my schemes to make it. One of my brilliant ideas that I had was to rob the KFC that I used to work at. Full on armed robbery in a ski mask. While working at KFC, I knew the late night procedure for closing the restaurant. I'd been there long enough to memorize the routine.

On late shifts, Calvin, my manager and the same former Navy guy who once punched me in the face for jerking off during dinner rush, would count down both registers at the end of the night. He'd then put all the cash in a small leather zip bag with a little lock on it and drive straight to the bank to make the deposit.

I had all the beats played out in my head. It was the perfect setup for an inside job.

The plan was simple: wait in the bushes outside of the KFC after closing and then jump out and stick up Calvin for the three to four thousand dollars in cash. I'd hide a screwdriver in my shirt, pretend it was a gun, and pop out from the shadows like, "Stick 'em up, motherfucker! Give me all your money!"

Looking back now, this plan was doomed from the very beginning.

I had a friend named Vinny lined up to be my getaway driver.

So, I got my screwdriver, grabbed a ski mask (which I, of course, stole from Modell's because I didn't want any proof of purchase), and had Vinny drop me off near the KFC. I crouched down in the bushes outside, waiting for the perfect moment.

When the lights inside finally went out, my whole body started shaking. I was literally shitting my pants in fear. My heart was pounding out of my chest. I watched Calvin walk out the back door, get into his car, and drive away.

And that was it.

I didn't even make an attempt. I just sat there in the bushes like a coward, frozen. There was nothing else to it beyond that. I simply didn't have the balls to go through with it.

And honestly, I'm really glad I didn't. There was no way in hell I was getting away with this. Calvin wasn't going to believe my screwdriver was a gun. He would've beaten the absolute shit out of me, ripped off my mask, and I would have gone straight to jail.

That's exactly how it would have played out if my better instincts hadn't taken over in that moment. Another really,

really bad life decision avoided—either by divine intervention or by momentary pussification. Either way, it worked out for the best.

Back then, I never really thought about the consequences of my actions. At that time, it seemed like stealing was more of a viable way to make money than any other option in front of me. And I was starting to get more and more involved in doing just sort of petty bullshit. For me, it started young.

We would go to the parking lot of supermarkets and get a receipt off the floor, when I was eight, nine, and ten years old. Go into the ShopRite, grab a box of Rice-a-Roni, or whatever was on the receipt, get it off the shelves, and go up to the cashier and say:

"My mom wants me to return this, here's the receipt." And get the cash for it. That's how it starts.

My mother was actually the first person to teach me how to steal. When I was very young, maybe seven or eight years old, she would take me to the local pharmacy called Baxter's. She'd point to the tester perfumes and tell me to swipe them for her.

She even coached me what to say if I got caught. "Just tell them it's your mother's birthday and you were trying to get her a gift," she'd say. "They'll think it's cute and let you go."

That was her logic, and at that age, I didn't question it.

Little things like that will desensitize you to things like stealing. It becomes a part of life. Even to this day, I don't feel this overwhelming moral objection to petty crimes like stealing. I feel like life presents opportunities and sometimes you gotta take them. Even if that means taking from someone else. I know that's not right, but it's just kind of built into my way of thinking.

It's not like I didn't know right from wrong. I did. My moral compass was just a little bit off. When I was a kid I would steal money out of my mother's purse, but I would never take dollar bills. Just coins. I had a line. I was willing to rob that KFC, but I never would have been violent with Calvin for a few thousand dollars. I wasn't willing to go there. Maybe that's why I didn't go through with it. I subconsciously knew that I wasn't willing to do what it took if shit hit the fan. Who knows? I just thank God I chickened out. I almost ruined my life.

## CHAPTER 23

# A NEW GENESIS

As you're already well aware, no one in my family has ever made any real money. No one. My mother never made more than a couple hundred dollars per week, and my Great-Aunt Anna Marie worked in a curtain factory named Hornick's for her entire adult life. She didn't have much, but she was responsible with what she had, so naturally she was the person everyone would mooch off of and take advantage of.

My mother would borrow money from her all the time and never pay it back. So would my uncles who were my mother's brothers. My uncles were all degenerates in one way or another. They varied in levels of their degeneracy. My aunt would get calls from them when they were in and out of jail asking for ten dollars here or twenty dollars there.

When I moved to the city, I didn't want to ever ask my Great-Aunt Anna Marie for anything. She was the person that everyone took advantage of, and I made a decision that I would never ask her for a handout. I hoped to one day be able to do the opposite, and do nice things for her.

When I first got to the city, I answered an ad in *The Village Voice*, an ad that, believe it or not, would eventually lead me down a path that would change my life forever. The ad read: "*Make $60–$150 a day. No experience necessary.*"

It was for an advertising company called Nu-Genesis Marketing Solutions. In reality, it was just two guys running sort of a hustle. They had secured a deal with the New York Comedy Club to promote and sell tickets on the street.

At the time, the New York Comedy Club was basically what could be considered a shithole club. Just grimy and broken down. It was owned by a guy named Al Martin, who, despite his shitty comedy club, was a decent enough guy.

I had just moved to New York and started at Baruch College on the first Monday of September 2001. But honestly, I barely went to class. I probably made it to a handful of lectures. I was only there for one semester. This was my second year of college, my first was at Rockland Community College, where I managed to pull my grades up just enough to get accepted to transfer to a school in the city.

In RCC, it was very lax. Just one or two classes per day. I remember trying to take a calculus class. I thought, "I know I am smart. If one person can do calculus, then so can I. I just need to actually pay attention and I'll be fine." By day three, I was completely lost. It was like they were speaking a different language. I passed pre-calculus in high school because I cheated and copied off of other kids. That's how I got through high school. By doing the bare minimum and just sneaking by.

At Rockland Community College, you had a week or two to drop and switch classes. So, I just loaded up on fun classes that I knew I could pass. I took an acting class, an art class, a tennis class, and a creative writing class and dropped the couple of classes that were above my head, like calculus. I just wanted to get through the year so I could eventually transfer to a school in New York City.

I really didn't move to New York for school. I was still dating Vicky, who was going to FIT, which is the Fashion Institute of Technology. I always thought it was kind of hilarious. Girls who were passionate about fashion seemed to be the dumbest girls on the planet. A whole college dedicated to brain-dead chicks who thought about clothes and shoes all day. I didn't really want to be in NYC, either. I just didn't want her to move to the city without me. So, really, I was just following her.

I chose Baruch College because, even back then, I knew I wanted to be in marketing. I wanted to be in business. I wanted to be an entrepreneur, and Baruch was offering those classes. But I hated college. The classes were ridiculously boring, and my head was really never into it to the extent it needed to be.

Very quickly I was cutting classes and playing hacky sack with other stoners outside of the school. I had a new problem, though—my weed habit was getting expensive. I was smoking a few blunts a day. Also, eating in NYC was pretty expensive, and I didn't even have money for the subway or bus to get around town. I would travel around on rollerblades.

To make money, I started scamming a little bit again. Baruch College was part of the City University of NY, or CUNY. There were maybe a dozen CUNY schools. Baruch, Hunter College, Borough of Manhattan Community College, and a bunch more. If you had an ID to go to one, you were granted access to all of the CUNY schools. I thought back to the scam I did when I was a kid, where we would find receipts in the supermarket parking lots and return items that were listed.

Every CUNY school had a bookstore that would buy back your used books throughout the semester. What I would do is just go into the store, grab a couple of new books, and sell them back to the store. I wouldn't even leave the store. I'd find an aisle with no one in it and I'd put the books on the ground and stomp on them to beat them up a little.

If you walked by it looked like I really hated reading. I did this at every CUNY school for the first week I was at Baruch. The problem was it was unsustainable. The same kids worked in the bookstore, and I could only return the books a couple times.

That's when I came across the ad in *The Village Voice*. I still remember going down to Broadway, just below Canal Street, for the interview. I almost missed it, and honestly, I almost gave up on the whole thing. I went to the wrong address. I wasn't on Broadway. I was on West Broadway which was a couple blocks west of Broadway. I just didn't realize there was a difference. I finally found the place an hour after the interview time was supposed to be. I was dripping sweat and very frustrated.

The company I was interviewing with would literally hire anyone. They didn't care who you were, as long as you were willing to try. The job wasn't just about promoting comedy shows, it was a full-on, belly-to-belly sales job. Commission based. You had to stop people on the streets of New York and pitch them: "Hey, what's up? Want to see a comedy show?" Or whatever your opening line was. The goal was to sell them a package of tickets, usually eight tickets for twenty dollars—with a six month expiration date.

Super cheap, super fast.

We would get paid 50 to 75 percent of our sales. A sliding scale depending how many tickets we sold on a given day. The company had an arrangement with Al Martin, the owner of the New York Comedy Club. He didn't want any of the money from ticket sales. All he cared about was that people came in and hit the two-drink minimum. That was his business model. We brought the bodies, and he made money off the booze.

And that was kind of it. From day one, I was unsurprisingly good at stopping people and getting them to buy comedy club tickets. Really good. It was essentially the same job I had when I was eleven years old hustling subscriptions for *The Rockland Journal News*. Most people (probably 90 percent) would quit almost immediately because they couldn't sell anything. They couldn't get people to stop and talk to them. On my first day, they put me on the same corner as another guy who had just been hired. This guy was tall, bug-eyed, and a bit grumpy. He barely tried to stop anyone and complained about how much this gig sucked.

I was stopping people left and right and he convinced me to bum some cigarettes for him. So, we just smoked cigarettes and shot the shit that afternoon. He didn't want to be doing the job. He was a comedian who had just moved from Philly, and he was just looking to get into some clubs.

That comedian's name was Kurt Metzger and I'm still friends with Kurt to this day. Kurt ended up being the guy that introduced me to Big Jay Oakerson, Nate Bargatze, Mike Vecchione, Joe DeRosa, and a bunch of other great comedians. Kurt quit the job after one day but we ended up linking up a couple years later once I started producing comedy shows.

Some people did stick around, but most of them couldn't make enough money to live on. So only a very small percentage of people could actually do this job at a level where they made real money. And by "real money," I mean that I was making around $500 a week right out of the gate. At that time, that was a lot of money for me. That was more money than anyone in my family had ever made by a lot. Something about sales just clicked for me. It resonated.

In Manhattan, it was easy to find targets. The hardest part of the job was getting people to stop and talk to you. Typically, they'd just blow right by you and ignore you. My strategy was to find people already stopped. People hanging outside of buildings, smoking cigarettes. I'd light one up too, and naturally ease into a conversation. From there, it became a sales process. You'd engage them with questions.

"Have you been to a comedy club?"

"How long will you be in town?"

"Who is your favorite comedian?"

Once you had enough information, you would "inform" them about your product. The idea was to match your product to all the information they already gave you.

Our comedy club was always better than the one they had been to. (It never really was. The New York Comedy Club was a real shithole, remember.) Their favorite comedian would "pop in all the time." (That never happened. No one of note was actually performing at the NYCC.) The tickets were good for six months, so it fit their schedule perfectly! "You must have a friend with a birthday in the next six months," I'd tell them. At that point, you'd close them.

They've already given you all the information you need. I wouldn't accept no for an answer. I was really good at getting around rejections. The guys who ran Nu-Genesis were actually pretty good at teaching sales to people who would apply themselves, and I actually learned a lot from that job. The sales process for selling a car or a house is essentially the same: Stop. Engage. Inform. Close.

After about a year and a half, I decided to branch out and start my own company, which I called PosterDog Promotions. At that point, I didn't need Nu-Genesis anymore. I had secured my own contract. In fact, I straight-up stole their contract with the New York Comedy Club.

At the time, Al Martin had just opened another club, The Improv, on the west side of the city, which would eventually become the Broadway Comedy Club. It was newer, nicer, and bigger. I asked Al Martin to let me take over the promotions for the New York Comedy Club with my team. The guys at Nu-Genesis didn't really push back on it. They were busy with the newer club. I saw the opportunity.

The truth was I basically lifted their entire business model. I knew I could do it better than them and I did do it better. I was the best at it. The best there is. The best there was. And honestly, probably the best there ever will be at that kind of street hustle. I understood early on that sales is a numbers game. Every no wasn't rejection, it was just part of the process. Statistically, every no brought me one step closer to a yes. If I was closing one out of every four people, then I knew I had to stop forty people to close ten. Most people would get discouraged after just one rejection. They'd get deflated, take it personally. But for me, every no was like progress, great, one step closer to money.

So, I'd actively chase the nos. I'd tell myself, let me get three rejections out of the way, and the fourth one's probably a yes. That mindset gave me energy, confidence, and from there, the rest was just having fun. Talking to people. Flirting. Trying to get girls to make out with me.

Funny story: When I first started selling tickets, I ended up becoming friends with radio legend Ron Bennington's daughter Gail. She was maybe sixteen or seventeen at the time, and me and my buddy Forrest, who was also my roommate, met her and a friend one afternoon. I had gone to high school with Forrest. He was a hippy and a pothead like me, and I convinced him to move to NYC after he flunked out of SUNY Albany. Gail and her friend started tagging along as we worked for a couple months. We'd smoke cigarettes and weed in Bryant Park. She never mentioned her dad working in radio.

Fast forward about twenty years, I was a guest on one of Ron Bennington's *Unmasked*, an in-depth interview show about your origins in comedy. I was telling a story about selling comedy tickets on the street when I noticed Gail giving me this weird look. I didn't recognize her at first, it had been so long.

Later, she DM'd me, saying, "I think we used to hang out when I was a teenager. Me and my friend would watch you guys work."

I replied, "Gail, I think we made out."

And she wrote back, "We definitely made out."

## CHAPTER 24
# NEVER FORGET

On the morning of 9/11, I had a four-hour-long marketing class at Baruch. It was a particularly boring class and particularly long. The class started at 8:00 a.m. and went to 12:00 p.m. with no break. The first tower was struck at 8:46 a.m. and the second at 9:03 a.m. They didn't let us out of class, so we had no idea the attack was even happening.

When I got out, I remember hearing an announcement over the PA system that said that classes were canceled for the rest of the day. I was like "Sweet! I can get high and play hacky sack!" I didn't notice the hundred or so students crying and freaking out around me. I was an idiot. My girlfriend Vicky's dad actually worked for the DEA, so he picked her up that afternoon and drove her directly out of the city.

They were not allowing civilian cars in or out. Vicky was Ukrainian and hid our relationship from her fairly strict Ukrainian parents. They wanted her to be with a Ukrainian boy, and she didn't want to deal with her dad knowing she was dating a poor Puerto Rican kid. So, she just left me. She told me I could stay at her room at the Chelsea Hotel (the same hotel that Sid Vicious from the Sex Pistols allegedly killed his girlfriend Nancy Spungen) that night, but I'd had to figure out a way home by myself. That was the moment I got over that relationship.

I stayed at the hotel that night feeling particularly depressed that my girlfriend left me. I raided her mini fridge and ate all of her Ramen noodles. The next morning, I woke up, strapped on my rollerblades, and decided that I had to make it back up to Rockland County. I had a cell phone, but all of the phone lines were down, so I had no way of communicating with my aunt or my sister. I rollerbladed from the Chelsea Hotel on 23rd street and 7th Avenue up the West Side Highway to the George Washington Bridge. That's roughly 150 blocks.

The city was a ghost town. It reminded me of a post-apocalyptic movie. Empty streets. Eerily quiet. No cars. No people. When I finally got to the GW Bridge, I knew I was maybe a third of the way home. I got a burst of energy, and started really moving. I didn't think about it, but when you get on and off the GW Bridge, there are rumble strips along the side of the road. I was really moving, and I went over the rumble strips, and it felt like my body was electrocuted. My entire body shook from head to toe.

Once again. I'm an idiot. I continued on across the bridge and up the Palisade's parkway. I had to get to exit thirteen which was the closest exit to my house. While I was roller-blading up the parkway, a red Volkswagen Jetta slowed down and the guy driving it asked me if I needed a ride. He was going up to Nanuet, which was a town a few towns away from

West Haverstraw. Fuck yeah, I wanted a ride. He dropped me off and I called my friend Vinny's home line from a payphone to come grab me. He showed up with a blunt already rolled and we got high as I tried to gather my thoughts and piece together what the fuck just happened.

When 9/11 happened, we took about a week off, but then we were right back out there, selling comedy club tickets on the street. At first, I cringed and thought, "No one is going to want to go to a comedy club right now. We were just attacked by terrorists." The funny thing is that New Yorkers have this great "Fuck You" attitude.

My first afternoon back I stopped so many people that were like "Yes! I will go to a comedy club. Fuck terrorism. I'm not going to stop living." I had people telling me how much they appreciated our efforts and that we were out there facilitating a good time. It was inspiring. I went to a comedy show at the club two weekends after 9/11. The club was packed. Every single comedian talked about the attacks. They all made jokes, and the crowd ate it up. They loved it. It was a beautiful thing.

Many of the people had lost friends and family members a couple weeks before. Lower Manhattan was still covered in ash. They were still looking for bodies. But everyone came together and laughed. It was another core memory for me, and it influenced how I do comedy today—making fun of fucked up things that are supposed to be dark and painful, and trying to find the funny in them. In my opinion, it is the way comedy should be done.

The MC of the New York Comedy Club, who was also the door guy, was the late Ozzy Baez. Ozzy wasn't very well known, but he had his act down. He knew how to kill a room. On this night, he had a few jokes fall flat. The logo for the NY Comedy Club was the New York City skyline crudely drawn and there was a sign with this logo on the wall behind the stage. After each joke Ozzy told that bombed, he made a gesture with his hand like a bomb was being dropped. He'd whistle and then make a bomb sound effect. After his third joke in a row bombed, he whistled but instead of the bomb dropping in front of him he flew his hand into the twin towers that were drawn into the logo. It killed.

After a month or two, I was making more money than anyone in my family ever had. And in my mind, I had made it. I truly believed I'd never need another job again for the rest of my life. I felt like I was on top of the mountain, like I had beaten the system.

I remember coming home one day and seeing my mom for the first time in a while. Ever since I got my driver's license, I had started leaving home for long stretches at a time. I would stay with James Meakim and his family up in Highland Falls, New York, or sometimes I'd crash at Dave Green's place with his family. Other times, I would just sleep in my car. Anything to avoid going back home. My relationship with my mom had completely deteriorated by this point. She had become really abusive, emotionally and physically, and it felt like she had just given up on everything—on herself, on parenting, on life in general.

She had cancer, and her vocal cords were damaged so badly she could barely speak above a whisper. It was like her body was shutting down, and she wasn't even trying to fight it. It felt like she was bracing for death instead of clinging to life. Years of chain-smoking cigarettes and doing hard drugs had finally caught up to her.

One night, I came back from the city. I took the bus from Port Authority up to Rockland County to spend the night at home. I was planning to meet up with some friends, smoke a little weed, and just chill like we used to.

At the end of the night, I went to my mom's place on Railroad Avenue. The apartment had a little front balcony, kind of like a small porch. It was late, she was already in bed, and I stepped outside to smoke a blunt. I was just sitting there, getting high, decompressing, zoning out.

When I finally came back inside, I heard her getting up from her bedroom. I panicked. I didn't want to deal with her. She had gotten so mean and bitter that any interaction could turn into a fight. I knew if she smelled the weed, it would be a whole thing. So I laid down on the couch and pretended to be asleep.

She came into the living room, and I kept one eye cracked just enough to watch her. I saw her glance at me, trying to see if I was asleep. Then she walked over, reached into the pocket of my jeans that were draped over a chair, pulled out my wallet, and started taking money from it.

I snapped awake and said, "What are you doing?"

She didn't have an answer. She looked ashamed, caught in the act. And I lost it. I completely exploded. Years of pain and resentment came rushing out like a dam breaking. I unleashed everything I'd been holding in for so long. I called her a piece of shit. I said horrible, vicious things. I told her I hoped she'd die of cancer, right to her face. It wasn't about that one moment. It was about everything.

I yelled, "Fuck you. I've had nothing in my life. You stopped buying me Christmas presents when I was twelve. You stopped supporting me. You stopped even pretending to care. I went out, got a job, started making my own money—and you have the balls to steal from me? You beat the shit out of me my whole life. You abused me. You failed me as a parent. And now that I'm finally doing something right, something for myself, you try to take that too? Fuck you."

That was the last conversation I ever had with my mother. I left the next day. A few years later, she passed away.

# CHAPTER 25
# WHITE POWDER

The first time I tried cocaine was September 4, 2001, exactly one week before 9/11. I remember the date clearly because it was the day System of a Down released their album *Toxicity*. That band basically became the soundtrack to all of my drug experiences.

It was my second day at Baruch College, and instead of going to class, I cut to buy the album and meet the band at Tower Records on West 4th Street. I had met members of System of a Down before. A couple years earlier, my crew and I had gone to Ozzfest. After the concert, Dave Green and I split off from the group and snuck around to where the tour buses were parked. That's when we ran into John Dolmayan, the drummer for SOAD.

He was incredibly friendly and approachable, just a genuinely cool dude. He invited us onto his bus to party with him and a few other rock stars. It was surreal. We were two teenage boys, and for five minutes, we were living the dream, until Rob Zombie had us kicked off the bus. I guess John forgot we weren't hot girls.

That moment always stuck with me. John seemed genuinely appreciative that we recognized him and were excited to meet him. I told myself that if I ever became famous, I'd be like that: available to fans, approachable. These days, social media makes that easier, but back then, getting even a quick interaction with a celebrity or rock star was rare and unforgettable.

I always think of the scene in Almost Famous where Russell Hammond, who is a massive rockstar, takes acid and goes to a house party with fans. He jumps off the roof into a pool yelling, "I am a golden God!" When I saw that, I remember thinking, "Yes, that's the kind of rock star I'd be. That's how you make memories people never forget."

Anyway, after I met the band that day and smoked a little weed, I was already feeling pretty good. Then I got a call from my buddy James Salcone, one of my older friends from Railroad Avenue. James had started getting into drugs more seriously. He was sniffing coke and heroin casually and also selling both. He'd drive into the city, buy them for twenty dollars a bag, then flip them in Rockland County for forty dollars to people who didn't know any better. My guess is most of his profits ended up going straight up his nose.

James told me he was coming down to the city for a pickup and asked if I wanted a ride back up to Rockland and to hang that night. I said "of course!" That bus ride sucked.

He picked me up, and we listened to *Toxicity* on the drive. I remember we were playing the song "Psycho"—a wild, fast-paced track about drugs and groupies. Right after that song, James pulled out a baggie of coke and asked if I wanted to try some.

By then, I'd already been smoking weed and had experimented with hallucinogens, but I'd never really dabbled in what I considered hard drugs. Still, I didn't have any strong aversion to it. At that point in my life, I was living a double life: on one side, I was hustling, stealing, smoking, and lying to my girlfriend. On the other, I was going to college, finding comedy, and trying to figure out who I was going to be as a man.

So, I said, "Fuck it. Let's do it."

James laid out four lines on the album cover and shaped them with his driver's license. Then he rolled up a one-dollar bill and went first: one line up each nostril. I followed suit.

The high was subtle. It wasn't like smoking weed or drinking for the first time. With those, you felt something good or bad. This? It felt like almost nothing. A little rush. I didn't get the hype.

James asked, "What do you think?"

I said, "I don't really feel anything.... Let's do some more!"

So, we did a few more lines. And that was really it.

Years later, though, I did end up getting pretty addicted to cocaine. It happened after my son's mother and I split up. I was depressed and started doing it alone. I hid it from all my close friends. I was looking for an escape.

That period of my life only lasted about a year, but it got dark. One weird thing about me is that whenever I do coke, I get a stye in my eye the next day. Every single time. I've talked about this on podcasts, maybe as a way to hold myself accountable. If you ever see me with a stye, just know, I probably have relapsed on cocaine.

## CHAPTER 26

# GOOD RIDDANCE

After I had moved to NYC my ex girlfriend Kristen showed back up. Randomly, I would see her. She had some problems. She would always confide in me, calling me from time to time to let me know what was going on with her.

The truth is, I always had a special place in my heart for Kristen. I felt bad for her. She was an addict. Her parents were addicts. It just had a hold on her. I had a few friends like that. My buddy James Salcone got addicted to heroin as well. Heroin is a terrible drug, and I've never tried it. I don't like needles at all.

I even considered getting on TRT, but the biggest deterrent was the needles. Kristen had some trouble with the law, too, mostly to support her habit. One time, she called me from jail. She'd been arrested for stealing the end-of-day deposit from a vitamin store she managed. Her plan was to just deposit an empty zipper bag and play dumb. She didn't think too much about it and was arrested and fired. Kristen wasn't a bad person. She just made bad decisions. I was very close to making similar mistakes.

When I was about twenty years old and living in Brooklyn with my friend Forrest, I got a call from Kristen. She and her boyfriend, some junkie whose name I don't even remember, were in the city and wanted to smoke a blunt.

Forrest and I were selling comedy club tickets at the time for my company, PosterDog Promotions, and had met a couple of girls earlier that day who were planning to come to our apartment to hang out. It wasn't weird. Kristen and I had broken up four years earlier and were genuinely just casual friends at this point, just checking in on each other here and there. So I said:

"Sure, come by. There will be some other people here."

The girl I was hanging out with was also named Kristen. In fact, her last name was Schulz, while my ex-girlfriend's full name was Kristen Schultz. Literally one letter off.

When ex-girlfriend Kristen showed up with her boyfriend, the girls were already at the apartment. We were all just getting high and listening to music. This was pre-smartphone, so we'd actually talk. No scrolling on your phone or making videos for TikTok.

Ex-girlfriend Kristen and her boyfriend were on something: pills or dope, something. They were both just falling asleep. New Kristen was a cool chick. Very cute and friendly. She had just moved to NYC from the Midwest or somewhere, and I might have been the first guy she went out with after getting to the city.

Everyone just kind of shrugged off their junkie behavior, and we went on partying and smoking. Ex-girlfriend Kristen and her boyfriend eventually left, and New Kristen spent the night. We made plans to see a movie the next night. This girl was pretty cool, and I was excited about it.

We met up around 5:00 p.m. and were walking around Union Square when she got a phone call from her father. I was kind of zoning out, but I heard her starting to get frustrated and upset during the call. She said something about her credit card being lost and not knowing where it was. I wasn't eavesdropping, but I was picking up little bits and pieces of the conversation.

She said, "I don't know what Adrian Arms is..." then, "Where is Route 304?" Then, "A smoke shop in Nyack, New York?"

She was naming places where I grew up in Rockland County. She hung up with her dad and explained that her father was pissed. Her credit card, which was really his credit card that she was an authorized user on, had been stolen. She wasn't sure how that could be possible.

Immediately, I knew exactly what happened to that credit card.

I told her, "Look, those are all places near where I grew up. I think my ex-girlfriend stole your credit card last night." Turns out I was still a rat.

She had to call her dad and explain to him that she went over to some random dude's apartment she met on the street while he tried to hustle her for comedy club tickets. Her dad wasn't happy, and I never saw New Kristen again.

As for ex-girlfriend Kristen, the story goes, she and her boyfriend went into New Kristen's purse while we weren't looking and stole her credit card. They knew that since their names were so close, ex-girlfriend Kristen could show her ID and use the card freely.

They bought gas, $500 worth of bongs and weed paraphernalia, and in the stupidest move ever attempted by a junkie, they tried to buy an AR-15 and ammo from a gun store. New York has very strict gun laws. They don't just hand you guns when you show up like they do in Texas or some other places.

So, ex-girlfriend Kristen and her boyfriend went in, signed the documentation and background check, and had to wait a week to come back and pick up the gun. In that time, the credit card had been reported stolen. The police were waiting for them at the gun store when they got back. They were both arrested.

To his credit, ex-girlfriend Kristen's boyfriend tried to take the complete blame, saying she had nothing to do with it. Unfortunately for her, she had signed for the gun and the credit card receipt, so she was fucked. They separated them and both were sent to a detention facility upstate.

While being transferred from jail to prison after he was sentenced, ex-girlfriend Kristen's boyfriend hanged himself in the police van with a seatbelt. I felt bad for Kristen. I knew her as a kid. But my actual gut reaction was:

"Fuck that guy. Good riddance."

A year later, I ended up hanging out with Kristen again one night while visiting Rockland County. She had gotten out of jail after a few months and was on probation. I hadn't seen her since that night. She had a sadness about her.

I asked if she wanted to smoke a bowl. Even though it was a violation of her probation, she said, “Of course I do. Here, use this.”

Then she pulled a bowl out of her glove box. It was mine. They had also stolen it from me the night they stole the credit card.

I was like, “What the fuck? You guys stole this from me!”

She said, “No, my ex gave this to me.”

“Yes, after he stole it from me,” I shot back. I was pissed. Then I threw the bowl out of the window of the moving car.

She looked at me with tears in her eyes. “Why would you do that? That was the last thing he ever gave to me.”

Then she broke down crying. I told her I felt bad, but I really didn’t.

Fuck that. Good riddance.

## CHAPTER 27

# SKANK ORIGINS

Dave Smith and I first crossed paths through the hustle of comedy club ticket sales. I was twenty-one years old, and at the time, I was casually seeing a girl named Katie, who sold tickets with me at Nu-Genesis and later went on to work for my company, PosterDog Promotions. Katie's best friend, Dina, had a younger brother named Dave who was looking for a summer job, so he joined our little crew as a promoter.

From the start, Dave and I just clicked. We had a similar energy and an easy way of getting along. We were both unapologetic potheads, chain-smoked Camel Lights, and pretty much lived off Heinekens. We didn't need much else to be happy. Hanging out with Dave felt natural, like we had been friends forever.

Dave and I ended up as roommates in a shitty two-bedroom apartment in Brooklyn. I basically lived on the couch, and another kid named Wes was staying there, too. Wes was a NYU student from a wealthy family. He was a jock, frat-bro type, and he's still a friend to this day. He later became a crypto-bro and is now a multi-millionaire. He always seemed destined to succeed. Dave was actually his roommate, and I needed a place to live.

A few months before that, I'd gotten a Jack Russell Terrier named Sport for my then-girlfriend, Alex, who was a super cute Polish chick with blonde hair, a big ass, and big tits. We were together for about three years.

We ordered the dog from a website called NextDayPets.com. You could literally have a puppy flown to you overnight. My buddy Gene drove me to the airport to pick him up. Gene was one of my old friends from Rockland County, and he's still part of the circle I keep in touch with today.

When I got the dog, I was living at the Manhattan Broadway Hotel on 38th Street, just off 8th Avenue. It was essentially a hooker hotel where you could pay by the hour or by the night. I couldn't get a proper apartment, because I had no credit and no savings for a deposit. I was living day-to-day, selling comedy club tickets, and paying about $1,200 a week to stay there. I had a few stints in that shithole.

So, there I was, living in a tiny hotel room with a brand-new puppy who pissed and shit all over the bed and puked on the floor. I had to get out. That's when I moved in with Dave and Wes.

We treated that apartment like it was a college dorm. I smoked two packs of Camel Lights a day, so the place was covered in cigarette ash and butts. Add in the weed smoke, and the whole apartment just reeked.

It was a third-floor walk-up, so we rarely took the garbage out. It would pile up and attract mice. One time, we were trying to find a mouse that had crawled into a bag of trash.

We were picking up each bag one by one and shaking them to see if they contained the mouse. At one point, one of the bags ripped open and garbage spread across the kitchen floor. The little mouse bolted across the pile and disappeared into one of the trash mountains. The garbage stayed on the floor for weeks and we never found that mouse. We were just a bunch of dirty-ass dudes living in a dirty-ass apartment.

Dave and I had already been friends for about a year when I started doing comedy; I wanted him to try it with me. At that point, I had been around the comedy scene for a few years, promoting clubs, producing shows, and figured, why not host my own show? I always had the itch to perform. I was the class clown in middle school and early high school. I just never admitted to myself that I wanted to do stand-up. I didn't want to say it out loud.

Dave was naturally funny. We'd get high and just laugh for hours, but he didn't want to go on stage yet. He kept saying: "I'm going to write the perfect five minutes first."

Which, of course, is dumb, you don't even know what stand-up is until you try it.

Our apartment was in Park Slope, right around the corner from a Blockbuster Video. We spent a lot of time there renting UFC DVDs. That's when we got into the UFC. Between me, Dave, and Wes (who was also a wrestler), we'd have grappling matches in our filthy living room—weed, beer bottles, cigarette butts everywhere. We'd wrestle until someone tapped out. I actually got cauliflower ear from wrestling Dave on that floor. If you see it today, it's not from jiujitsu training, it's from what we jokingly called the Gomez-Smith

Fighting System, or the Smith-Gomez Fighting System, if you asked him.

At the same time, I was producing comedy shows and booking killer comics. Kurt Metzger introduced me to a lot of the Philly guys like Joe DeRosa, Mike Vecchione, and Big Jay Oakerson. I also started working with Nate Bargatze, who would eventually become my son's godfather, and New York legends like Todd Barry and Jim Gaffigan.

I've always had a good eye for talent. Even back then, I knew Kurt and Big Jay were high-level comics. They were only five or six years in, which is still baby years in comedy, but they were already killers on stage. Looking back, maybe I should've felt intimidated trying to do stand-up alongside those guys, but I didn't. I believed in myself. I truly thought I could do anything I committed to.

My first sets were just random thoughts and crowd work. I started hosting shows and relied on charisma, flirting with girls from the stage, and getting them to flash their boobs for drinks. I remember my first joke.

I'd say, "You guys want to see an impression of Elvis?"

Then I would cross my arms over my chest and close my eyes like I was dead. The audience would groan.

Then I'd say, "OK, but seriously, you want to see Elvis Presley, if he were alive today?"

Then I'd knock on the mic as if I was trapped in a casket. "Hey, somebody let me out! It's really dark in here!"

It got laughs. That was my first bit.

Eventually, I started developing an actual set. I started off doing silly bits, but eventually I started talking about real shit, more serious and darker topics. Trying to find the funny in that type of subject matter challenged me and it was the type of comedy that I enjoyed.

I always wanted to be honest with the audience. Nothing was off-limits. That goes back to 9/11, when comics started joking about it, I realized comedy could turn tragedy into laughter. That became a core part of my voice. The stuff you cry about in therapy I turned into material, and that process gave me thick skin.

Even now, on podcasts where we're constantly busting balls, I have the thickest skin in the room. Back in the early days, I probably wasn't mature enough as a comic to dive into my personal pain, but those years laid the groundwork. Back then, it was all raw personality and ringleader energy. Over time, that foundation evolved into the darker comedy I'm known for today.

It's wild to see how people evolve. When I first got Dave into comedy, he wasn't political at all. Now, he's one of the smartest political commentators in the world. But back then, he was what I'd call a wigger. He grew up in Brooklyn, hung out with Black and Latino kids, smoked blunts, and drank 40s on the stoop. He was scrappy, though. If someone messed with you, he was ready to fight by your side. We spent a ton of time together. We were roommates, but we also worked together selling comedy club tickets. During the summertime, selling tickets was actually a pretty sweet gig. New York City is alive in the summertime. It was easy to get tourists to stop and talk to you on a nice sunny day.

Selling tickets in the winter sucked. It was impossible to get people to stop and talk to you in freezing cold weather.

We'd keep it simple. We'd try to make forty dollars for the day, which was enough for a twenty dollar bag of weed, two 22s of Heineken, and a pack of smokes. Just two twenty-dollar sales. That was the goal. We would work for an hour until we couldn't take the cold anymore, then we'd find a building with an open door and take a break in the stairwell. We knew all of the buildings that left their doors open and didn't have doormen or security. There was this one building on 8th Avenue between 38th and 39th called The Music Building that was our favorite. It was an entire building of studios that you could rent to rehearse music. Musicians all smoked weed and dressed like degenerates, so we were able to slip in and out unnoticed. The door was always open. We'd go up to the top floor and smoke blunts between hustling tickets.

It was like a real-life, toned-down version of the movie *Kids*, minus the AIDS. It was around this time when I first started to hang out with Big Jay outside of comedy. I remember a group of comics went to see *Star Wars Episode II: Attack of the Clones* at a midnight showing. I think it was me, Jay, Jamie Kilstein, Pete Holmes, Kurt Metzger, and maybe a couple others.

After the movie ended around 3:00 a.m., Kurt and I had to get back to Brooklyn. We hailed a yellow cab. Kurt had gone to 7-Eleven and bought a giant 64 ounce Slurpee. We told the driver where we were headed, and he said:

"No, I'm not taking you."

He was an Arab guy with a thick accent. It's illegal to refuse a fare so we pushed back. I said "Fuck that man. You're taking us." We got in the car and refused to get out. He had no choice but to start driving. The driver was eerily quiet while he was driving. He was supposed to get off for the exit for the BQE and he ignored it. Just drove past it not saying anything. We told him he missed it, but he just ignored us. At that point, we were both scared but didn't want to admit it, so we acted tough: "Motherfucker, you better turn around!"

He just kept driving.

"Pull over! Pull over!" Finally, he did.

We got out, and Kurt started writing down his cab ID number. Kurt said: "Yeah, motherfucker, we're going to get you fired!"

Then, in a moment of defiance, he threw his Slurpee at the cab, aiming for the driver's window. The window was barely cracked and Kurt didn't have great aim. The Slurpee hit the window and it bounced and ricocheted back toward Kurt. It hit him square in chest. He was covered in ice cold Slurpee from head to toe. The cabbie laughed his ass off and drove away. We never reported him.

One of the things that me and Big Jay connected on early was the game *Guitar Hero*. We were obsessed. One time, Jay invited me over to his apartment in Queens to play. He and his girlfriend, Carla, (the mother of his daughter and future ex wife) ended up getting into a huge argument when I was there. Jay was cheating and she knew it. During one of their fights, she screamed at him:

"Why don't you go hang out with your legion of skanks?!"

Me and Jay looked at each other and raised our eyebrows. He said, "That's a great band name!"

Originally, "Legion of Skanks" was just our *Guitar Hero* band. Now it's obviously become so much more. That name came straight from Big Jay's pissed-off girlfriend, and it turned out to be gold.

Jay has always been funny on a higher level than most. He's fluent in the language of funny. It doesn't matter if he's in a car, on stage, doing crowd work, or telling a story, he makes people laugh. He performs at the highest level in comedy.

Interestingly, Jay only smoked pot three or four times in his life before he started hanging with me. I 100 percent turned him into a pothead, so maybe I wasn't the best influence. But pot aside, I got to witness his development as a comic up close. He started out in Philly with Kevin Hart. They even toured as "Big Jay and Little Kev."

Watching your best friends become mega stars forces you to step your game up. It stops being about just getting laughs, and it becomes about building a real act. Not just a set, but an identity you can tour the world with and build an audience.

Jay went from being happy just getting stage time to becoming one of the most respected comics in the world. Watching that transformation was incredible.

In the early days, everything was about making each other laugh like we made each other laugh in middle school at the lunch table. I think that's what finding your "voice" is. Like in its purest form. Why did your friends find you funny growing up? Can you bottle that up? Can you execute and make strangers see it?

In the beginning it was more pure. It was just about laughs. After you achieve some success, you start to manufacture things a little bit. "Write that down," or "Save it for the podcast." The natural, chaotic funny dissipates as it becomes a business.

Ironically, it's kind of sad.

# CHAPTER 28
# SUCK AND F*CK

For most of my adult life, I was a pothead. I didn't just smoke weed, I based my whole personality around it, and I was proud of it. Back when it was illegal in NYC, I probably got arrested nine or ten times for smoking on the streets, usually around Washington Square Park near NYU. The NYPD would run sweeps of the park, picking people up for public urination, smoking weed, drinking from open bottles, petty stuff like that. And whenever my friends and I got caught, the cops would always take me in and let my White friends go. The cops would be like:

"Well, we have to take one of you."

And guess who that "lucky one" always was?

They'd toss me into a paddy wagon with a bunch of other kids, who, unsurprisingly, were all Brown people, and drive around picking up more until the van was full. Then they'd bring us down to the local precinct to check for outstanding warrants, fingerprint us, and process us. From there, they'd pack us into another paddy wagon and send us to central booking in downtown Manhattan, where you'd sit in a giant holding cell waiting to see a lawyer or a judge.

The first time I was there, I was terrified. I had no idea how long the whole process would take or what was going to happen. But by the sixth or seventh time, it had almost become fun, in a weird way. I knew I'd be out of there within twenty-four hours, as long as I didn't go in on a Friday night. That was the rule: If you got picked up on a Friday, you weren't seeing a judge until Monday, so you were stuck all weekend. Thankfully, I never had to do that stretch. I think the longest I ever spent in the holding cell was thirty or thirty-five hours.

The cell itself was old and filthy, with a toilet bowl sitting right in the middle of the room, and there'd be fifteen to twenty other people crammed in there with you. A lot of times, people would smuggle in weed and rolling papers and sell joints inside. You'd spend fifty bucks for a joint and another twenty just for a match to light it. Same thing with cigarettes. Every time I was in central booking, I'd end up buying menthol Kools or Newport's. That's why anytime you went into the system, you made sure you had a little cash on you, especially if you knew it was going to be a longer stay.

So yeah, I loved weed, and I was willing to chill out in central booking every now and then if that was the price I had to pay for doing what I loved. Which is exactly why, once I started to put a little money in my pocket, the first obvious travel destination I wanted to hit was Amsterdam. The weed capital of the world. So, me and some friends got our passports, hopped on a plane, and headed over.

We lit up at the very first place we saw where you could legally smoke weed. We were staying in Utrecht, a city about a half-hour outside of Amsterdam, so we'd have to take the train in every day to get to Amsterdam proper. But the second we got off the train, there was this little Jamaican run weed shop with smoke billowing out of it. There was even a scruffy black cat just chilling outside like the place's unofficial mascot.

It was me, Dan Doherty, Gene Kelly, and this kid Jake, who none of us really liked that much. We only invited him because he had a credit card to book the trip and hotel on. We ended up charging room service to his card the entire trip and never paying him back.

Being able to legally smoke weed for the first time was awesome. We'd get high, then head straight to the red-light district to see hookers. I was with two different hookers while we were there. They were gorgeous and cheap! "Fifty Euro suck and fuck," they'd say. I didn't have a lot of money on me, maybe a couple hundred euros total for the four or five nights we were staying, so by the last day, we were completely broke.

We found this small café and figured we'd grab some sandwiches with the maybe twenty euros each we had left. I'm a New Yorker, so when I'm thinking sandwiches, I'm thinking big. Like a fat meatball hero or a loaded Italian sub, something you need two hands to eat. But the only option they had was ham and cheese sandwiches, which was fine, we thought, because we assumed they'd be big enough to hold us over until we flew out.

I ordered one and figured, I'll eat half now and save the other half for dinner. Dan and Gene did the same. But when the sandwiches came out, they were these tiny little European finger sandwiches. Like you could finish one in three bites. I looked at my sad little sandwich and said:

"Fuck it. I'm not paying for this. I'm going to dine and ditch."

Gene immediately agreed: "Yeah, fuck this place. Dine and ditch."

But Dan Doherty, who was very neurotic, started panicking. He said, "No, we're not going to dine and ditch! We're going to pay for it, and that's that!"

We told him, "Dude, we're leaving. In fact, we're going to run. So, if you want to stay behind and pay for everyone, go ahead, but we're out of here."

Dan was still protesting, "No, man, don't do it, we're not running!"

But before he could finish the sentence, me and Gene were already sprinting out the door. Dan had no choice but to get up and follow us. He didn't have enough money to pay for everyone's meal.

I remember we ran about four blocks before we had to stop and catch our breath. We were stoned plus none of us were in shape, and we were dying. While we were standing there hunched over, gasping for air, we looked up and realized we had made four left turns. We were now standing directly in front of the same café we had just run out of.

Right on cue, one of the workers stepped outside, pointed at us, and said, "Excuse me…"

And we just bolted again. No hesitation. We didn't stop running until we were far away. Somehow, we made it to the airport the next morning and flew back to New York, broke, exhausted, and still laughing about the whole thing.

# CHAPTER 29

# I FORGIVE YOU

I guess it was maybe a day after returning from Amsterdam that I was back on the streets of Manhattan selling tickets when I got a phone call from my aunt. And for some reason, the second I saw her number pop up, I just knew. My mother was dead. I knew it before she even said a word. My aunt didn't call me that often, and as soon as I saw her name on the screen, I felt it in my gut. It was pure intuition.

When I answered the phone, my aunt began to speak, and that intuition was confirmed.

I remember not feeling any real emotion in that moment. Nothing. I think, deep down, I always knew this was coming. It felt inevitable, something that was going to happen sooner rather than later. My mom had been diagnosed with cancer back when I was in middle school. And I'd mentioned earlier in the book that the last time we'd spoken, we got into a huge argument, and I told her, to her face, that I wanted her to die of cancer.

So, when I got the news that she had officially passed away, I wasn't happy. I wasn't relieved. But I also wasn't crying. I was just completely emotionless. Like I'd been expecting this moment for years and it had finally arrived. I hung up the phone and went right back to selling tickets like nothing had happened.

About a week later, I went to her funeral. No one had any money for a headstone, a nice casket, or beautiful flower arrangements. It was me, my sister, a few other family members, and then all these junkies my mother had known. And in that moment, it became clear to me that my mother had been using drugs again. My aunt had been kind of hiding the truth from us, telling everyone she'd died of cancer when, in reality, it was a heroin overdose.

After pressing my aunt further, she finally admitted the truth. She also told us that the police implied that it wasn't an accidental overdose. That she had committed suicide with heroin. Life finally caught up with her. In the end, she was too far gone. Too depressed. Unable to speak and in physical pain. She didn't have the will to keep going.

Years later, I'd struggle with guilt over that. I felt like maybe it was my fault, even though I knew deep down it wasn't. That's something I've had to work through in therapy. I thought, maybe if I hadn't been so wrapped up in my own life at the time—if I'd spent more time with her, checked in on her more—maybe she wouldn't have been in such a deep depression. But the truth is, I'll never know.

It is what it is.

The first time I cried about her death was on the day of her funeral. I went up to the coffin. It was a closed coffin, and the shittiest, most run-of-the-mill coffin you could get, and I put my hand on it and just started crying.

My aunt, who's not good with emotions, came up to me and said: "All right, come on, let's go."

And I had a moment of rage, like, let me just fucking be here for a minute. All these suppressed emotions were coming back up. It was the anger and years of abuse and frustration, and maybe having some regret that I didn't fix things with her while she was still alive. I had unanswered questions. What if I had been more understanding and forgiving of her, and what if she wasn't just so shitty to me my whole life?

I had an overwhelming feeling like it didn't have to be this way, and a deep regret that now there was no way to make right all the things that went wrong. She had a tough life. She was a kid, just eighteen years old when she had my sister, and twenty when she had me. She was sexually and physically abused her entire childhood. She was addicted to heroin, and the father of her children was murdered. It was a fucked-up life by any metric.

My mom had become bitter, angry, and still abusive, but also sad, like a shell of her former self. When she was younger, she had this bright personality. After my dad died, for a few years, she really tried to give us a suburban life. Even though we were on welfare and Section 8, and she was still abusive and unstable, there were flashes where she tried to be a good mom. She signed me up for the Boy Scouts and Little League baseball. She spent every last cent she had in the world to bring us to Wrestlemania XI.

There were a few years where she really did try. She'd bring cupcakes to my class on Halloween, volunteer to chaperone field trips, and show up to PTA meetings. It was only a short stretch of time, but it felt longer to me. When you're a kid, those moments seem bigger, especially when they become memories of someone who's gone.

She died when I was twenty-two. I left home around sixteen and only went back in short visits before eventually moving to New York City. I was staying with girlfriends, crashing on couches, doing whatever I could to avoid being around my mother. It was partly because she was mean, but also because she was just…sad. My sister's relationship with her deteriorated, too.

The truth is, we all kind of felt like she gave up. It was like she killed herself slowly with the drugs. And honestly, I understand that. For a while, I used drugs too.

After the breakup with my son's mother, I was depressed. I used to the point where I didn't care if I died. So, I get that mindset. After all the loss she went through, I can see how she got there. I have empathy for that person.

My mother was ready to go. She refused treatment. Stopped taking care of herself. She smoked the entire time she had cancer. She never quit, not even for a day. It's like she just wanted to go out that way.

She made a lot of bad choices. But between the cancer, her mother dying, and her kids pulling away from her, I think she just lost the will to live. That's how she died—without speaking to me, and having a tumultuous violent relationship with Jeni.

She wrote me a bunch of letters, but I never had the courage to read them. I lost them while moving between apartments. My sister read them before she gave them to me. She told me they were filled with apologies. Apologies for being who she was, for being abusive, for everything.

There's one thing she gave me after we stopped talking. It was for my twenty-first birthday. A framed poem you'd buy at Walmart or CVS. I still have it in my kitchen.

The poem is called "For If I Could Love You More." Then, on the back of it, written in her handwriting, is the only message I have left from her:

> *April 2003*
> *Happy 21st Birthday*
> *I love you, wish you all the best that life has to offer. May you find the path to all your dreams, because if anyone can do it you can. I'm so proud of the man you've become. I couldn't ask for a better son.*
> *Forgive me, please.*
> *Mom*

Everyone has someone in their life who's passed away. Someone you wish you could sit down with one last time, just for a moment. Maybe to say something you never got the chance to say. Maybe to just sit in silence and exist together for one more breath.

I've always tried to live my life with no regrets. I opened this book by saying I wouldn't change a thing, and I meant that. Every fucked-up moment, every painful memory, every hard lesson was part of the same path that led me here. And I love where I'm at. I have a son I'm proud of. A career I built from nothing. A life that I never thought I'd have. So yeah… no regrets.

The good, the bad, the brutal, the beautiful, it all had to happen exactly the way it did to make me into the man I am. Life doesn't give you do-overs. It gives you scars. And sometimes those scars become the foundation for everything strong in you.

I'm not a spiritual person. I don't know what comes after this. But on the off-chance that I'm wrong, and my mom is somewhere out there, maybe even reading this, somehow, I just want her to know…

"I forgive you."